MUNZ, PHILIP
INTRODUCTION
CALIFORNIA DESERT
2004.

37565001134666

PETA

P9-DLZ-949

OFFICIAL
DISCARD

CALIFORNIA NATURAL HISTORY GUIDES

INTRODUCTION TO CALIFORNIA DESERT WILDFLOWERS

California Natural History Guides

Phyllis M. Faber and Bruce M. Pavlik, General Editors

Introduction to

CALIFORNIA DESERT WILDFLOWERS

REVISED EDITION

Philip A. Munz

Edited by Diane L. Renshaw and Phyllis M. Faber

UNIVERSITY OF CALIFORNIA PRESS

Berkeley   Los Angeles   London

California Natural History Guides No. 74

University of California Press
Berkeley and Los Angeles, California

University of California Press, Ltd.
London, England

© 2004 by the Regents of the University of California

Library of Congress Cataloging-in-Publication Data

Munz, Philip A. (Philip Alexander), 1892–
    Introduction to California desert wildflowers / Philip A. Munz; edited by
Diane L. Renshaw and Phyllis M. Faber.—Rev. ed.
        p. cm. — (California natural history guides ; 74)
    Rev. ed. of: California desert wildflowers / Philip A. Munz. 1962.
    ISBN 0-520-23631-9 (case) — ISBN 0-520-23632-7 (pbk.)
        1. Wild flowers—California—Identification. 2. Desert plants—California—
Identification. 3. Wild flowers—California—Pictorial works. 4. Desert plants
—California—Pictorial works. I. Renshaw, Diane L. II. Faber, Phyllis M. III.
Munz, Philip A. (Philip Alexander), 1892–
California desert wildflowers. IV. Title. V. Series.

QK149.M788 2004
582.13′09794—dc22   2003060433

Manufactured in China
10   09   08   07   06   05   04
10   9   8   7   6   5   4   3   2   1

The paper used in this publication meets the minimum requirements of
ANSI/NISO Z39.48–1992 (R 1997) (*Permanence of Paper*). ⊚

Cover: Sand verbena and dune primrose, Anza-Borrego Desert
State Park. Photograph by Christopher Talbot Frank.

The publisher gratefully acknowledges the generous
contributions to this book provided by

the Gordon and Betty Moore Fund
in Environmental Studies
and
the General Endowment Fund of the
University of California Press Associates.

CONTENTS

EDITOR'S PREFACE
TO THE NEW EDITION

Introduction to California Desert Wildflowers has introduced thousands to the wildflowers of the desert areas of California. Since it was first published in 1962, a number of plant names have been changed, and, in some cases, new information has been obtained. In this revised and updated edition, a number of steps have been taken to make the book current in content and appearance.

The first step was to review the selection of plants included. Philip Munz was most at home in the California deserts, and his expert knowledge of those regions is reflected in his original choices for inclusion in this field guide. After careful consideration we decided to retain Munz's original selections, without additions or eliminations.

Dr. Robert Ornduff wrote introductions to all four of the newly revised Munz wildflower books before his untimely death in 2000. His introduction to this volume describes the environmental factors that shape the desert habitat, and discusses some of the adaptive strategies that allow plants to survive in the harsh extremes of that setting.

Scientific names for each plant have been made to conform to the current California authority, the *Jepson Manual: Higher Plants of California,* J. Hickman, editor (University of California Press, 1993). In addition, almost every plant in this edition has been given a common name using the following sources, listed here in descending order of preference: the *Jepson Manual;* Philip Munz, *California Flora* (University of California Press, 1959); and Leroy Abrams, *Illustrated Flora of the Pacific States* (Stanford University Press, 1923–1960). Because some of the desert plants are not well known, occasionally it was necessary to consult additional sources (Philip Munz, *A Flora of Southern California;* and Willis Linn Jepson, *A Manual of the Flowering Plants of California*) to find an acceptable common name. In several instances there was no alternative but to use a proper name or surname in the common name, and in a few cases there simply was no common name found that would apply to the plant being described.

The rule developed by Munz for hyphenation has been used for all common names: If a plant's common name indicates a different genus or family, a hyphen is inserted to show that the plant does not actually belong to that genus or family. Thus, "skunk-cabbage" is hyphenated because the plant it refers to is not in the cabbage genus nor the cabbage family, but "tiger lily" is not hyphenated because the plant it refers to is in the lily genus, as well as the lily family. Within each color section the species accounts are arranged according to the same taxonomic order used by Munz in his original edition of *Desert Wildflowers.*

In the original edition of this guide, Munz called the two major deserts of California the Colorado Desert and the Mojave Desert. The new *Jepson Manual* no longer recognizes the Colorado Desert as a separate section of the larger Sonoran Desert, but to avoid any misinterpretation of Munz's original plant distribution accounts, this revised edition has retained the use of "Colorado Desert" as a more specific regional indicator.

Taking into account research done in the last 50 years, some species have been absorbed into other species, and some have been split into varieties or subspecies. Some varieties or subspecies have even become separate species. Each plant description has been carefully checked and revised or rewritten as needed for accuracy and currency. Some of the author's original language was out of date. An effort has been made to retain the Munz intent yet to make the new edition readable, entertaining, and informative to today's readers.

Diane Renshaw has brought the scientific names up to date and has made necessary and appropriate revisions and additions to the 1962 plant descriptions. The Press is grateful to her for her meticulous work. Many of the lively drawings of Jeanne Janish, mentioned in Munz's introduction, have been retained. New color illustrations and new design features have been added to make the book more user friendly. The Press is especially grateful to Jon Mark Stewart for sharing his outstanding collection of accurately identified color slides, many of which appear in this book, and for his patience in the revision process.

Many of the plants found in this book have had their range severely reduced by habitat destruction and disturbance and by invasive weeds. Users of this book are urged to respect all native plants and refrain from picking or collecting specimens. Please enjoy our unique flora, but leave it to flourish for future generations.

Phyllis M. Faber
April 2003

ACKNOWLEDGMENTS

Most of the drawings used in this book were made by various graduate students working at the Rancho Santa Ana Botanic Garden: Dick Beasley, Stephen Tillett, and Shue-Huei Liao. Others were by Helen G. Laudermilk. Still others by Milford Zornes, Rod Cross, and Tom Craig were used in 1935 in my *Manual of Southern California Botany,* which has been out of print for many years. This book was copyrighted by Claremont College, and I wish to thank President Robert J. Bernard of that institution for permission to reproduce these drawings now. The Kodachromes belong to the collection of the Rancho Santa Ana Botanic Garden, many of them having been taken by Percy C. Everett. It is a pleasure to acknowledge the help of all those mentioned above and of Gladys Boggess in preparation of manuscript.

Philip A. Munz
June 1961

The Rancho Santa Ana Botanic Garden at Claremont, California, was established for the study of the native plants of California. When in 1959, after about 12 years of continuous work, the large technical book *A California Flora* (Munz and Keck, University of California Press) was published, it seemed to me that the Botanic Garden as an institution and I as an individual owed something to the general reader not trained in botany but interested in his surroundings in nature. I therefore planned a series of three small books that could be placed in the glove box of the car or carried easily when on a hike. These books were to consist primarily of pictures, some as ink drawings and some as color photographs, with just enough text to give names and a few pertinent facts describing the plants and their location. The young man who made most of the drawings for the first of these three books suggested the catchy title *Posies for Peasants* and caught exactly the idea of a nontechnical approach I imagined.

The California Deserts

The California deserts comprise a considerable area if we include the region below the yellow pine belt *(Pinus ponderosa)*, beginning in the north with the lower slopes of the Sierra Nevada and a large part of the Inyo and White Mountains and their environs and ending in the south with the Imperial Valley and the arid mountains to the west and the sandy region toward the Colorado River. Roughly, and for practical purposes, we can think of our desert as consisting of (1) the more northern Mojave Desert reaching as far south as the Little San Bernardino and Eagle Mountains and the ranges to the east and (2) the more southern Colorado Desert. Being quite different from each other, these two deserts are worth short separate discussions.

In the first place, the Mojave Desert, except for the Death Valley region and the area about Needles, lies mostly above

2,000 feet. Hence, it has more rainfall and colder winters. It opens out largely toward the northeast and in many ways is an arm of the Great Basin of Utah and Nevada, and its plant affinities often lie in that direction. The Colorado Desert, on the other hand, consists largely of the Salton Basin, much of it near or below sea level. It opens toward the southeast, and its affinity floristically is with Sonora, and it is often placed as part of the Sonoran Desert. Not surprisingly, then, many species of the Mojave Desert extend into Nevada and southwestern Utah, whereas many of the Colorado Desert range into Sonora and western Texas. There are of course many patterns of more limited distribution, such as along the mountains bordering the western edge of the Colorado Desert from Palm Springs into northern Baja California or around the western edge of the Mojave Desert from the base of the San Bernardino Mountains to the Tehachapi region.

The climatic conditions in the desert and the situation for plant growth are severe. Plants have had to resort to interesting devices to exist at all. In the first place, seeds of many desert plants have so-called inhibitors that prevent germination unless the inhibiting chemicals are thoroughly leached out by more than a passing shower. This means that for many of them it takes a good soaking rain to get started, one that wets the ground sufficiently for the seedling to send a root down below the very surface. A second characteristic of many of the annuals is that if the season is rather dry, they can form a few flowers even in a most depauperate condition and ripen a few seeds under quite trying circumstances. Thirdly, many of those plants that do live over from year to year cut down evaporation by compactness (small fleshy leaves and reduced surface area as in cacti), by coverings of hair or whitish materials that may reflect light and hence avoid heat, and by resinous or mucilaginous sap that does not give up its water content easily, as exemplified by creosote bush *(Larrea tridentata)* and cacti.

A widespread popular fallacy should be mentioned. We read of the great depth to which desert plants can send their roots in order to tap deep underground sources of moisture. This situation is true along washes, watercourses, and basins, where mesquite *(Prosopis glandulosa* var. *torreyana)* and palo verde *(Cercidium* spp.), for example, send roots down immense distances, but in the open desert an annual rainfall of six or eight inches distributed over some months may moisten only the upper layers of soil. Therefore, shrubs such as creosote bush and plants such as cacti tend to have very superficial wide-spreading roots that can gather in what moisture becomes available.

Something should also be said about summer rains. On the coastal slopes at elevations below the pine belt, we are accustomed to summer months practically without rain. But in Arizona and the region to the east of us, there are two definite rainy seasons: one producing a spring flora and another producing a late summer and early fall crop. For the most part the annuals that come into bloom in these two distinct seasons are quite different. Many summers, the Arizona rains reach into the desert areas of California and sometimes produce veritable cloudbursts of water. At such times thunderheads appear over the adjacent mountains such as the San Bernardino, San Jacinto, and San Gabriel Mountains, and the neighboring coastal valleys are much more humid and uncomfortable than when the desert is dry. After these summer rains some of the perennials may exhibit new growth and flowering, and a new crop of annuals may appear, such as chinchweed *(Pectis papposa* var. *papposa)* and California kallstroemia *(Kallstroemia californica)*. In the southern Mojave Desert west of Baker and Cronise Valley, I have seen the desert floor green for miles with California kallstroemia in early September.

As any desert habitué knows, plant life there is not uniform but varies with elevation, drainage, character of soil, and the like. One of the characteristic features is the presence of many undrained basins, known locally as "dry lakes," where water may gather in unusually wet years only to dry up more or less completely after a few weeks. Such a situation through the centuries brings about the accumulation of salts or alkali, making these areas too salty for any plant life, or at the fringes there may be an accumulation of species adapted to salty conditions, such as various members of the goosefoot family (Chenopodiaceae), including desert-holly *(Atriplex hymenelytra)* and iodine bush *(Allenrolfea occidentalis)*. These basins are scattered over the Mojave Desert and form a series along the old channel of the Mojave River, which flows eventually into Death Valley, the largest of all. A similar situation exists in the area near the Salton Sea.

The great open plains and flats of much of the desert are covered with creosote bush (which is associated with burroweed *[Ambrosia dumosa]*), box thorn *(Lycium cooperi),* brittlebrush *(Encelia farinosa),* and many other species. Here the average rainfall is from two to eight inches, and summer temperatures may be very high. Some cacti grow in this region, which is mostly pretty well drained, but many are found on rocky canyon walls, in stony washes, and in other places also. In areas above the creosote bush in the Mojave Desert, say from 2,500 feet to 4,000 or higher, Joshua trees *(Yucca brevifolia)* tend to distribute themselves in a sort of open woodland with lower shrubs in between. Here the annual precipitation may be from six to 15 inches, and the vegetation is correspondingly richer. And then, along the western edge of the Colorado Desert and more particularly in the mountains bordering on and situated in the Mojave Desert, is a zone of pinyon and juniper, mostly at 5,000 to 8,000 feet. Here the annual precipitation runs about 12 to 20 inches a year, some of it as snow. This belt has some summer showers and some plants in bloom in summer and even fall, as well as in spring, which comes later than in the creosote bush zone. Particularly in the more northern parts of the desert, creosote bush gives way in the upper elevations to sagebrush *(Artemisia tridentata* and relatives), and large regions in Lassen, Mono, and northern Inyo Counties have a sagebrush desert like that of Nevada and Idaho. With so wide a diversity of conditions, then, it is not surprising to find quite different flowers at various altitudes and in various habitats.

How to Identify a Wildflower

It is impossible to talk about plants and their flowers without using some specialized terms to describe their parts. Some of the most necessary terms are explained here, and a more complete list is defined in the glossary. In the typical flower we begin at the outside with the sepals, which are usually green, although they may be colored. The sepals together constitute the calyx. Next comes the corolla, which is made up of separate petals, or the petals may grow together to form a tubular or bell-shaped corolla. Usually the corolla is the conspicuous part of the flower, but it may be reduced or lacking altogether (as in the grasses [Poaceae] and sedges [Cyperaceae]), and its function of attracting insects for pollination may be assumed by the calyx. The calyx and corolla together are sometimes called the perianth, particularly when they are more or less alike. Next, as we proceed inward in the flower, we usually find

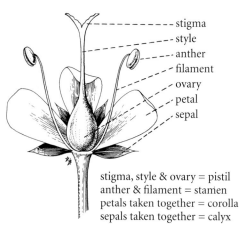

stigma
style
anther
filament
ovary
petal
sepal

stigma, style & ovary = pistil
anther & filament = stamen
petals taken together = corolla
sepals taken together = calyx

The parts of a representative flower

the stamens, each consisting of an elongate filament and a terminal anther where the pollen is formed. At the center are one or more pistils, each with a basal ovary containing the ovules or immature seeds; a more or less elongate style; and a terminal stigma with a rough, sticky surface for catching pollen. In some species, stamens and pistils are borne in separate flowers or even on separate plants. In the long evolutionary process by which plants have developed into the many thousands of types of the present day and have adapted themselves to various pollinators, their flowers have undergone very great modifications, and so now we find more variation in them than in any other plant part. Our modern system of classification is largely dependent on the flower parts.

To help with the identification of a wildflower, either a color photograph or a drawing is given for every species discussed in detail, and the flowers are grouped by color. In attempting to arrange plants by flower color, however, it is sometimes difficult to place a given species to the satisfaction of everyone. The range of color may vary greatly, from deep red to purple, from white to whitish to pinkish or greenish, from blue to lavender, or through a wide range of yellows and oranges, so that it presents a challenge for the writer himself, let alone the readers, to determine whether one color group or another should be used. I have done my best to recognize the general impression given with regard to color and to categorize the plant accordingly, especially when flowers are very minute and the color effect may be caused by parts other than petals. My hope is that by comparing a given wildflower with the illustration it resembles within the color section that you think is most correct and then checking the facts given in the text, you may, in most cases, succeed in identifying the plant.

One of the chief difficulties in writing such a book is to find usable common names. I am not interested in taking those coined from the scientific name by a professional botanist who breaks down the genus name into its Greek roots and then adds the species name, such as, for example, the common name Mrs. Ferris's club flower for *Cordylanthus ferrisianus*. On the other hand, if the local inhabitants call this bird's beak, that is acceptable. For some plants, however, I may have been unable to ascertain a true folk name. In these cases it has seemed best to me to use the genus name, such as *Phacelia* or *Oxytheca*, as a common name too. Many desert plants are not very conspicuous and just do not have good, widely used names, so we have to resort to this scientific appellation.

Another problem I confronted is which plants to present. I have tried for the most part not to include those already shown in *California Spring Wildflowers*, so that anyone having both books has that many more species shown. I have chosen plants that I feel are interesting, but not all are necessarily showy or common. I have attempted not to present the various closely related forms of a complex group but have taken one as an example and often added a word about additional forms closely resembling the first. I have tried, too, to include species from the different parts of the desert so that the book is useful for more than just the Palm Springs region, for example, or just Death Valley, to name two of the commonly visited areas.

I cannot help but register a plea that residents of the desert and visitors thereto exercise discretion in picking, transplanting, and otherwise interfering with normal development and reproduction of desert plants. The thousands of people who live in or visit the desert nowadays are bound to inflict hardship on the vegetative covering. With the scant rainfall, desert plants grow slowly, and a branch broken off a pinyon tree for a campfire may have taken many years to produce. Certainly those who have known the desert over a period of years cannot help but be appalled by the magnitude of the recent destruction.

Philip A. Munz
Rancho Santa Ana Botanic Garden
Claremont, California
June 1, 1961

INTRODUCTION TO THE PLANT COMMUNITIES OF CALIFORNIA'S DESERTS

Robert Ornduff

The word "desert" brings to mind dry, hot, harsh landscapes that scarcely support living beings. By definition, deserts are harsh environments, but California deserts support a surprisingly rich diversity of plants and animals. Three major deserts occur in the state: the Mojave Desert, the Colorado Desert, and the Great Basin Desert. The wildflowers described in this book grow in the first two deserts. Plants of the Great Basin Desert, found east of the Sierra Nevada and Cascade Range crests, are not included. Philip Munz's introduction to the first edition of this book, which is reproduced here, describes the location of the Mojave and Colorado Deserts in California, gives a brief account of their climates, and presents a synopsis of representative adaptations of the plants that live in these extreme environments.

The term "desert" has no precise definition; a desert is simply an area with low average annual precipitation. Deserts may occur along coastlines, in interior regions, at the poles, or on mountaintops. They may be very local, lying in the rain-shadows of mountains; they may occupy the uppermost peaks of mountains; or they may extend over many thousands of square miles, as does the Colorado Desert, which is a northwestern extension of the vast Sonoran Desert. Portions of the Mojave and Colorado Deserts receive an annual average precipitation of four inches or less. In places, some years pass with no measurable precipitation. In parts of our deserts, rainfall is mostly limited to winter months, but in other areas there are two peaks of rainfall—one in winter and another in summer. The Mojave and Colorado Deserts have high numbers of sunny days during the year—commonly more than 300 days per year are cloudless or nearly so. Summers are hot, with 150 days or more having maximum temperatures exceeding 90 degrees F. Death Valley may be the hottest place on earth—a maximum temperature of 134 degrees F has been recorded there. Winters in our deserts generally are mild. The Mojave Desert is wetter and cooler than the Colorado Desert because it occupies higher elevations. It may even experience frosts or light snowfall during winter. The Mojave Desert occupies about two times more area in California than does the Colorado Desert.

Plants that grow in deserts must be able to survive extended drought and low annual precipitation and must be able to survive relentless heat and intense sunlight. California deserts by no means offer a uniform environment. Soils vary from place to place, and there are local occurrences of gypsum, alluvial fans, dry washes, oases, and soils with various levels of salinity. As one ascends desert mountains or descends into desert valleys, climatic and soil conditions change in relation to elevation, and these changes are reflected by differences in vegetation types and plant communities. The higher elevations may support juniper and pinyon pine woodlands; the lowest elevations are often highly saline and support only a few plant species. In low areas where the soils are moderately saline, low shrubs with intriguing names such as winter fat (*Krascheninnikovia lanata*), burrobush (*Hymenoclea salsola*), and hop-sage (*Grayia spinosa*) predominate. In even lower, highly saline areas that are the dry beds of former Pleistocene lakes, alkali sink scrub predominates. Here one finds the odd succulent shrub called iodine bush (*Allenrolfea occidentalis*) (because its sap stains human skin brown) and the equally succulent pickleweed (*Salicornia* spp.). The prominent American botanist T.H. Kearney once wrote of these shrub-dominated communities that "no other vegetation…gives the impression of being so nearly conquered by the environment," and even Philip Munz, author of this book, admits that these shrublands cover "large monotonous areas." Yet many visitors to the desert find this so-called monotony appealing and come back every year to enjoy its peaceful visual simplicity.

Two woody plant species occur over large parts of the California deserts. The more widespread of these is creosote bush (*Larrea tridentata*), which grows over about 16 million acres of the Colorado Desert and the lower elevations of the Mojave Desert in California. Creosote bush is the most abundant and widely distributed woody plant in the warm deserts of North America; it ranges from the southwestern United States to Guatemala, and close relatives grow in the deserts of southern South America. Creosote bush, sometimes called greasewood, is a dense evergreen shrub with leaves and branches that have an odor reminiscent of creosote. It thrives in hot, dry areas from below sea level to about 4,000 feet; the species is intolerant of saline soils and is damaged or killed by prolonged subfreezing temperatures. Because it is so common, creosote bush is often considered an uninteresting plant, but its dark evergreen foliage, resinous fragrance, and small but copious yellow flowers that are followed by tiny fuzzy fruits all add to the olfactory and visual interest of this sturdy species. Creosote bush shrubs are seemingly almost immortal. As they grow in diameter through the centuries, the central portion of the shrub dies, leaving a ring of free-living shrubs around this central area. The shrubs in this ring are all members of a single clone. Based on estimates of clonal growth rates, one enormous creosote bush clone called the King Clone is believed to be about 12,000 years old.

The higher edges of the Mojave Desert are occupied by vast tracts of Joshua tree woodland. Joshua tree (*Yucca brevifolia*) may not be considered a typical tree by some because of its bizarre appearance, but it is tall and woody and usually has a single central trunk and aerial leafy branches. If that doesn't qualify this species as a tree, what should we call it? Joshua tree, like all yuccas, has an interesting relationship with a specialized pollinator, the so-called yucca moth. If you visit Joshua trees or other yuccas when they are in flower, you will notice very small, whitish, day-flying moths flitting around the large masses of white flowers. These are Joshua tree yucca moths, whose life cycle is tied intimately to that of the Joshua tree, and vice versa. The female moth collects pollen from the anthers of the flowers, rolls the pollen into a small ball, and carries it using specialized mouthparts. The female then lays eggs on the ovaries of the female yucca flowers and deposits the ball of pollen grains on the stigma at the tip of the style. The pollen grains germinate, and the ovules are fertilized, eventually developing into seeds. Meanwhile, the moth eggs have hatched, and the larvae have burrowed into the ovary, where they feed on developing seeds. The young do not devour the entire seed crop but only enough seeds to allow them to mature and provide the next generation of moths that emerge when the yuccas next come into flower. At the same time, the yucca flowers have been pollinated and produce sufficient seeds to maintain the yucca population over the decades.

The low annual rainfall and high daytime temperatures that characterize California deserts provide inhospitable conditions for plants as well as animals. In his book *Travels with Charley,* John Steinbeck wrote, "I find most interesting the conspiracy of life in the desert to circumvent the death rays of the all-conquering sun." Desert animals are motile and can rest in burrows, crevices, or the shade of desert shrubs during the day to avoid the heat. Some of these animals venture forth after sundown, when temperatures are low, to feed and sip dew. Some desert animals have very low water requirements or can obtain water from their food. Plants, on the other hand, cannot hide during the day to avoid heat and cannot move about in search of moisture. Plants use water to maintain turgor and thus their characteristic architecture (a wilted plant lacks turgor) and as a medium in which the chemical reactions of metabolism take place. They also use water to move dissolved minerals and foods throughout their tissues and as an essential component of the complex set of chemical reactions called photosynthesis.

Desert plants possess an impressively wide variety of mechanisms that enable them to make economical use of the extremely limited water supplies in desert environments. One of the most familiar mechanisms for economizing on water is that employed by succulent plants. These absorb water through their shallow root systems after a rain and store it in their stems, leaves, or both during the very long dry spells between rains. The most familiar succulents in California deserts are members of the cactus family such as fishhook cactus *(Mammillaria tetrancistra),* various species of cholla and prickly-pears (*Opuntia* spp.), and hedgehog cactus (*Echinocereus engelmannii*). As adult plants, these cacti lack leaves and store water in fleshy stems that are usually armed with spines. Most plants, even in deserts, have leaves and carry on photosynthesis in the leaves, but because cacti lack leaves, photosynthesis is carried on in the stems, which are green because of the chlorophyll contained in their surface cells. The stems of cacti can expand and contract like accordions as water is taken up and later gradually used by the plant. Under experimental conditions, some cacti have survived without being watered for several years. A 10-foot specimen of saguaro cactus *(Cereus giganteus)* in Arizona that was deprived of water for three years weighed 48 pounds at the end of that period. After three weeks of rain, the plant had taken in so much water that its weight nearly doubled to 86 pounds.

The ferocious spines that cover the surface of most of our cacti ward off thirsty herbivores (if you encounter a cholla, resist the temptation to touch it, even gently, or you will find your fingers full of tiny transparent needlelike spines that are difficult to see and to remove). Spines may also shade the plant surface, reduce air movement along the surface and thus reduce water loss, help drain away heat from the stems, and even direct drops of nighttime dew to the soil at the base of the plant where its roots can absorb it. Although cacti often show few signs of life during the year, their flowers are frequently very large and colorful. Century plant (*Agave* spp.) and live-forever (*Dudleya* spp.) are also succulents, but they are not cacti; they store water in their fleshy leaves rather than in their stems.

Cacti and other succulents may be locally abundant in California deserts, but there are relatively few species of these plants in our deserts, and they do not dominate vast tracts of land. As one goes eastward into Arizona or southward in Mexico, cacti and other succulents become a more conspicuous feature of desert landscapes. Far more numerous in California deserts are more conventional-looking nonsucculent shrubs and perennial herbs. They do not store water but have other ways of economizing on the scant water supply. Creosote bush and Joshua tree belong to this group, as do numerous perennial herbs such as locoweed (*Astragalus* spp.), scarlet gilia (*Ipomopsis arizonica*), verbena (*Verbena* spp.), and Panamint daisy (*Enceliopsis covillei*).

The diversity of ways by which this group of perennial, nonsucculent plants cope with a scanty water supply is almost overwhelming. Many of these plants have waxy coatings on their leaves; this coating waterproofs the plants and reduces water loss from the leaves. Many species have dense hairs on the leaf surfaces, often to the extent that the foliage is gray or white. These mats of hairs reduce water loss by trapping moisture next to the leaves or by reducing the drying effects of desert breezes. Their light coloration also reflects some of the hot rays of the sun away from the leaf surface, which results in reduced water loss. Other species, such as Mormon tea (*Ephedra* spp.), have tiny leaves, and most of the photosynthesis is carried on in their green (but not succulent) stems. Some species, such as the evergreen shrub jojoba *(Simmondsia chinensis)*, have leaves that are vertically oriented and present a minimal surface area to the direct rays of the sun. Other species, especially grasses, have the ability to roll up their leaves during a hot day, thus reducing surface area and forming a tube that helps reduce water loss. Some woody species such as ocotillo *(Fouquieria splendens* subsp. *splendens)* are drought deciduous, that is, when soil moisture levels fall below a critical level, the plant loses its leaves. When heavy rains fall, new leaves are produced and the plants may even flower. If watered continuously in the garden, ocotillos are evergreen, but under field conditions they are not. Blue palo verde *(Cercidium floridum* subsp. *floridum)* is also leafless during much of the year, but as its common name indicates, it has chlorophyllous bark and can carry on photosynthesis even when leafless.

In photosynthesis, carbon dioxide, water, and light combine to make energy-rich sugars. This process requires movement of water into the plant via the roots and its transport throughout the stems and leaves. In order for photosynthesis to occur, carbon dioxide gas must move from the atmosphere into the interior of the plant, and oxygen, one of the products of photosynthesis, must leave the plant's tissues into the surrounding air. Movement of these gases occurs through tiny apertures called stomates that perforate the surfaces of leaves and stems. They also allow precious water to be lost from the plant's tissues. Stomates are surrounded by cells that open and close them. Plants typically have open stomates during the day because that is when gas exchange associated with photosynthesis occurs, but open pores also result in water loss. Some desert species have the ability to close stomates during the day; these plants open their stomates at night when temperatures are cooler and humidity is higher so that water loss is reduced. The plant takes in carbon dioxide at night, which is then converted into organic acids that are stored in the plant tissues and gradually converted back to carbon dioxide, which is used in photosynthesis during the day when the stomates are closed. Plants with this unusual type of mechanism include cacti and other succulents and members of the spurge (Euphorbiaceae) and sunflower (Asteraceae) families.

Some desert plants carry on a version of photosynthesis in which there is enhanced efficiency in the use of carbon dioxide and water, thus reducing the need for water and the risk of water loss during daylight hours. These plants have high optimal temperatures for photosynthesis, up to 115 degrees F, a temperature that would disable conventional photosynthesis. Photosynthesis of these plants also has a high light saturation, light levels that likewise would disable conventional photosynthesis. This type of photosynthesis occurs in creosote bush, many desert perennials, summer annuals, and many members of the grass (Poaceae), goosefoot (Chenopodiaceae), and sunflower families.

Desert plants may have very shallow root systems that fan out from the plant body only a few inches below the soil surface. These roots take advantage of the moisture that accumulates in upper soil levels after rain. A few desert plants, especially the trees and shrubs that grow along desert washes, have deep root systems that penetrate up to 180 feet below the soil surface and tap underground water tables. An example of such a deep-rooted species is mesquite *(Prosopis glandulosa* var. *torreyana),* which does not look like a desert plant because its aboveground parts resemble those of species found in areas with high rainfall. These deep-rooted desert plants have no obvious adaptations to drought because they have access to a continuous supply of water deep in the ground. Unfortunately, in parts of the Colorado Desert where underground aquifers have been tapped for human use, mesquite trees have died because the water tables have dropped too low for their roots to reach. California fan palm *(Washingtonia filifera)* is a remnant of a tropical flora that once occurred in California but disappeared because of climatic changes. This impressive tree is limited to oases in the desert, where there are permanent springs.

One interesting phenomenon that reduces competition

among desert plants is called allelopathy (this has also been termed "chemical warfare" among plants, but that dramatic term does not describe how it works). Many desert shrubs such as creosote bush synthesize organic chemical molecules that are exuded from their tissues and permeate the surrounding soil. These compounds are toxic and prevent seedling establishment of potential competitors in the immediate vicinity of the plant that produces them. The result is that allelopathic plants often are widely spaced, looking as if humans have planted them in orchards. This wide spacing is an effect of allelopathy and gives allelopaths nearly exclusive access to soil moisture and nutrients in their immediate vicinity. In a spring following heavy winter rains the ground among allelopathic shrubs may be carpeted with annuals. The roots of these annuals are restricted to the upper soil layer from which the allelopathic chemicals have leached by the rains. Because they are annuals, however, they do not pose a long-term threat to the well-being of their allelopathic companions because they are present on the site only during a brief period of late winter and early spring.

In late winter every year I receive telephone calls from friends and colleagues around the country asking, "How will the desert be this spring?" What these callers want to know is how abundant and well-spaced winter rains were and if the deserts will burst into flower during spring break. My usual answer to these inquiries is that despite the nature of the winter rainfall, I cannot predict whether it will be a colorful spring until the plants themselves come into flower. These natural flower shows are produced by winter annuals, plants whose life span is counted in weeks and who spend most of the year as seeds rather than as living, growing, flowering adults. During a wet year these annuals provide dazzling mats of color in our deserts, beginning in the low, hot desert of the Anza-Borrego Desert State Park area east of San Diego and ending several weeks later in the higher cooler deserts of Joshua Tree National Monument.

Winter annuals germinate, grow, and reproduce when soil moisture levels are ample and when daytime temperatures are relatively cool. Once the soil dries out and temperatures begin to rise, the plants quickly produce seeds and die. During the hot, dry summer, these winter annuals are not in evidence but persist as seeds. Because these annuals that have average moisture and temperature requirements die with the onset of the hot, dry summers, they are called drought evaders. Some winter desert annuals are known to have special seed germination requirements. Their dormant seeds must be subjected to a minimum of half an inch of rain before they will germinate. Presumably thousands of years of desert life have genetically imprinted on these annuals that half an inch of rain offers reasonably good assurance that the rest of winter will be wet enough to allow them to flower and set seeds normally. Upon germination, the seedlings may produce two seed leaves and appear to cease growth, but during this period the young plants are establishing extensive root systems that enable them to capitalize on whatever scanty rainfall comes their way. Then the seedlings may produce a rosette of leaves that lie flat on the ground. This ground-hugging feature places the leaves in a position where they receive maximum daytime warmth on cool winter days and may also help in reducing water loss from the leaves. With the onset of spring and the prospect of declining rainfall, the rosettes of many species produce surprisingly large, brilliantly colored flowers. These provide the showy floral displays that attract so many visitors to California deserts in early spring. These showy winter annuals include lion-in-a-cage *(Oenothera deltoides)*, whose large white flowers open in early evening and are visited by hawkmoths. After the plant dies, the stems curl inward to form an odd basketlike tumbleweed that detaches from the soil and rolls around the landscape scattering seeds. This explains the fanciful name for this unusual plant. Other evening-primrose species produce smaller white or yellow flowers, but en masse these can be showy. Monkeyflowers

(*Mimulus* spp.) come in shades of pink and purple. Desert sand-verbena *(Abronia villosa)* is deep rose. Tackstem *(Calycoseris wrightii)* bears a white daisy, coreopsis (*Coreopsis* spp.) and desert-dandelion (*Malacothrix glabrata*) bear yellow daisies, and tidy-tips *(Layia platyglossa)* produce bicolored yellow-and-white daisies. Some desert annuals attract attention not because of their showy flowers but because of their curious architecture. Desert trumpet *(Eriogonum inflatum)* is so named because its tall flowering stems are shaped like an upright trumpet. Desert candle *(Caulanthus inflatus)* is a curious plant with inflated erect stems.

There is a small group of desert annuals whose seeds germinate after heavy summer thunderstorms when air and soil temperatures are high. For the most part these summer annuals have inconspicuous flowers and do not provide the massive shows of their winter counterparts. Because few human visitors venture into California deserts during summer, these summer annuals largely go unseen.

Other lifestyles are known in desert plants. A number of attractive shrubs and small trees occur along the beds of desert washes. These washes are dry during most of the year but become filled with torrents of fast-moving water after rainstorms. Once this surface water disappears, the subsurface soil holds moisture for long periods of time, hence the relative lushness of this riparian community. Many of the plants that grow in this habitat have seeds with very thick coats. When the watercourses are flooded, the tumbling of the rocks abrades the seed coats so that germination and seedling establishment can occur while the soil is still moist. A few desert species have deep underground bulbs and produce leaves and flowers only during a few weeks in spring and early summer. During the prolonged summer, the plant is represented only by a fleshy bulb that resides deep in the relatively cool soil. Desert plants with bulbs include desert lily *(Hesperocallis undulata)*, blue dicks *(Dichelostemma capitatum* subsp. *pauciflorum)*, and desert mariposa *(Calochortus kennedyi)*.

Some colonies of the latter species do not produce leaves or flowers during a dry year, and one instance is known of a population that did not produce any flowers or leaves for seven dry years in succession. Plant parasites are also found in the deserts. Mistletoes (*Phoradendron* spp.) grow on the branches of junipers and various shrubs. Paintbrushes (*Castilleja* spp.) obtain nutrients by attaching themselves to the roots of other plants, though they also carry out photosynthesis in their leaves. One of the most curious desert parasites is sand food *(Pholisma sonorae),* which resembles a fleshy toadstool but is a true flowering plant. Sand food grows in sand dunes.

Visitors to California deserts often express surprise to find ferns growing in these areas because normally ferns are associated with moist, cool, shaded habitats. Many desert ferns behave as so-called resurrection plants. During wet periods, the leaves are green and carry on photosynthesis. As the soil dries out, the leaves appear to die, but in reality they are merely curling up as they become desiccated and enter dormancy. When the next rain falls, these dry plants take up water and the leaves unfurl, turn green, and resume photosynthesis. Cloak fern *(Cheilanthes parryi),* lip fern *(Cheilanthes covillei),* and desert goldenback fern *(Pentagramma triangularis* var. *maxonii)* all behave this way, as do the related little club mosses *(Lycopodium clavatum).* These plants are not flowering plants but reproduce via minute spores.

Paradoxically, although our deserts are harsh environments, desert ecosystems are fragile ones. Various types of off-road recreational vehicles have done seemingly permanent damage in many areas of the desert. Mining, overgrazing by feral animals such as burros and horses, overgrazing by domestic animals, industrial and residential development, military activities, aggressive introduced weeds, and agriculture have all had their negative impacts. Fortunately, large tracts of our deserts now are protected as state and national parks or monuments.

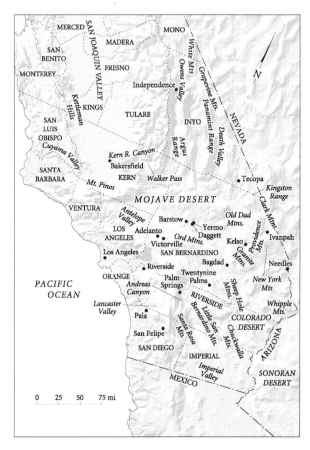

Map of desert regions

Cloak fern

Ferns do not reproduce by flowers and seeds but typically have rounded or elongate sori on the undersurface of the leaves. Instead of producing many-celled seeds, the sori release one-celled microscopic spores. Ferns are usually associated with fairly moist situations and are not commonly expected in the desert. Ferns are there, however, and they are most apt to be found under overhanging rocks and in rock crevices, where they are shaded, can make full use of the scanty rainfall, and are protected from browsing. One of the most common desert ferns is **CLOAK FERN *(Cheilanthes parryi)*,** a low, tufted plant in the brake family (Pteridaceae). The leaves have a light gray or brownish wool on their undersurfaces and are borne on wiry purplish brown petioles or stipes. Cloak fern is found at elevations below 7,000 feet from the White Mountains to the Colorado Desert.

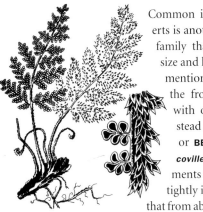

Common in the California deserts is another plant in the same family that is about the same size and habit as the previously mentioned species but with the fronds covered beneath with overlapping scales instead of wool. It is **LIP FERN**, or **BEAD FERN, (Cheilanthes covillei).** The individual segments of the frond are so tightly inrolled at the margins that from above they look like little green beads. Lip fern is found in rocky places below 9,000 feet.

The **DESERT GOLDENBACK (Pentagramma triangularis var. maxonii)** is a third fern in the brake family that grows in low tufts. Its frond is wider in proportion to length than are those of cloak fern (Cheilanthes parryi) or lip fern (C. covillei), and it is covered beneath with yellowish or whitish powder instead of being woolly or scaly. All three of these ferns are apt to be found in rocky canyons such as those near Palm Springs. During the dry season they roll up tightly and form dusty little clumps. (See photograph, page 26.)

Similar to the ferns in not producing flowers and seeds but instead multiplying by single-celled spores are plants in the spike-moss family (Selaginellaceae). These plants belong to the genus *Selaginella.* Our California species are low or creeping, with minute, scalelike, overlapping leaves. The tips of

Desert goldenback

Desert selaginella

some branches have the leaves slightly modified, bearing solitary spore cases in their axils. Often we can see these only by bending the leaves away from the stem. On the desert we have two of the most characteristic species of spike-moss. **DESERT SELAGINELLA** *(Selaginella eremophila)* is the more common of the two. It has stems that lie quite flat on the ground and occurs below 3,000 feet in canyons along the western edge of the

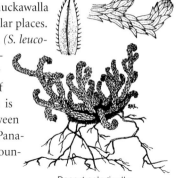

Colorado Desert, in the Chuckawalla Mountains, and in other similar places. The other, Mojave selaginella *(S. leucobryoides)* (not shown), is cushionlike and distinguished by having a bristle at the tip of each leaf. Mojave selaginella is found in rocky places between 2,000 and 7,500 feet in the Panamint Range and Providence Mountains, and in similar ranges.

Desert selaginella

The cone-bearing plants are the next major taxonomic group of plants after the ferns and their allies. Common on the dry, rocky slopes and flats rising above the desert are cone-bearing trees, including singleleaf pinyon pine *(Pinus monophylla)*, California juniper *(Juniperus californica)*, and Utah juniper *(J. osteosperma)*. At somewhat lower elevations over most of the desert are the distantly related shrubs from the Mormon tea, or ephedra, family (Ephedraceae). The species shown here is **NEVADA EPHEDRA (Ephedra nevadensis)**. All ephedras have jointed stems and scalelike leaves in groups of two or three, depending on the species. Typically, plants are either female, producing seed-bearing cones, or male, with clusters of pollen-shedding stamens projecting above the small cone scales.

Nevada ephedra

Fringed onion

In the lily family (Liliaceae) is a large group of plants with a bulbous root and an onion or garlic odor collectively known as wild onion. One of the most common species in the desert is **FRINGED ONION** *(Allium fimbriatum)*. The outer coats of its rounded bulb are dark, the leaf is solitary and rounded in cross section, the flower cluster is compact, and the flowers

Thurber's spineflower

are rose to purple with darker midveins. The many forms of this species vary in height, but most extend only a very few inches above the ground. Fringed onion is found in the desert on dry slopes and flats between 2,000 and 8,000 feet and to the west into the Coast Ranges.

In the buckwheat family (Polygonaceae) we have **THURBER'S SPINEFLOWER** *(Centrostegia thurberi),* an erect annual, forked above, with basal leaves. The flowers are very small and contained in an involucre with three spreading basal horns. These involucres are often quite highly colored and terminate at the summit with spine-tipped teeth. The species is common throughout our deserts in dry, sandy places below 7,000 feet. Its range extends to the east into Utah and Arizona and to the north and west into San Benito County. Flowering is from April to June.

HOP-SAGE *(Grayia spinosa),* in the goosefoot family (Chenopodiaceae), is a gray green shrub, often spiny, with small, somewhat fleshy leaves. The two bracts that grow around the female flower are united into a conspicuous, reddish, reticulate sac, almost half-an-inch long. Sometimes these bracts are more white than red, and so this plant is also mentioned under "Whitish Flowers." Rare in the western Colorado Desert, hop-sage is common in the Mojave Desert between 2,500 and 7,500 feet and ranges northward to Lassen and Siskiyou Counties and into eastern Washington, Wyoming, and Arizona. The small flowers appear from March to June. (See photograph, page 32.)

Hop-sage

FRINGED AMARANTH (Amaranthus fimbriatus) is a handsome annual in the amaranth family (Amaranthaceae) and is related to another amaranth, garden cockscomb. This common desert species has numerous narrow leaves and slender, erect stems up to two feet high. The many small flowers clustered on the stems lack true petals but instead have rose or lavender sepals that are fimbriate or coarsely fringed on their margins, making conspicuous masses of color. Found in dry, gravelly places below

Fringed amaranth

Desert sand-verbena

5,000 feet, fringed amaranth occurs from the Colorado and eastern Mojave Deserts to Utah and Mexico. It is a fall plant.

Sand-verbenas are not true verbenas at all but belong to the four o'clock family (Nyctaginaceae). **DESERT SAND-VERBENA (Abronia villosa)** is one of the more common species, a much-branched, hairy, often sticky annual with stout stems that can be almost two feet long. The clusters of purplish rose flowers are about half-an-inch long, subtended by narrow bracts, and very fragrant. The fruit is hard, with wings, and the base of the flower tube remains attached, making a small hook. The plant is common in open sandy deserts and interior coastal valleys, extending eastward to Nevada and Sonora. It flowers from February to July.

Also in the four o'clock family is a remarkable coarse perennial herb called **STICKY RING,** or **RINGSTEM,** *(Anulocaulis annulatus).*

This plant has one or perhaps a few stems, one to three feet tall, ringed with transverse, sticky, reddish brown bands between the leaf nodes. Small, stiff hairs on the stem have an enlarged, dark, glandular base. The open inflorescence has slender branches that end in headlike clusters of small pinkish to greenish flowers. Sticky ring grows in sandy and gravelly places below 3,000 feet in the Death Valley region and blooms in April and May.

Another member of the same family is **WINDMILLS,** or **TRAILING FOUR O'CLOCK,** *(Allionia incarnata),* a perennial or winter annual. The rose magenta flowers are about half-an-inch or more in diameter, scattered along the viscid stems in clusters of three. Found on dry, stony benches and slopes below 5,000 feet, windmills is a characteristic plant of both deserts, ranging eastward to Colorado and Chihuahua. Flowers appear from April to September.

FROEBEL'S FOUR O'CLOCK *(Mirabilis multiflora var. pubescens)* is yet another representative of the four o'clock family and the largest native species in the genus *Mirabilis.* Growing from a thick, woody, tuberous root, it forms sprawling masses that are hairy viscid throughout, although occasional plants are quite smooth and not sticky. Froebel's four o'clock has broad leaves, one to three inches long; the rose purple to deep pinkish flowers, one to two inches long, are arranged with several in a common green involucre. Found in the deserts in dry, stony places below 6,500 feet, this four o'clock ranges westward to San Luis Obispo and San Diego Counties and northward to Mono County. It flowers from April to August.

Windmills, or trailing four o'clock

Froebel's four o'clock

WESTERN SEA-PURSLANE *(Sesuvium verrucosum)* is a native desert plant in the fig-marigold family (Aizoaceae), formerly known as the iceplant or carpetweed family. It is a rather fleshy, freely branched perennial with stems almost flat on the ground. The spatulate, fleshy leaves are in opposite pairs, with the flowers in their axils. The sepals are purplish to rose pink, with transparent margins. It is not a beautiful plant but is quite common, especially in more or less saline places. Flowers appear from April to November.

The desert surprises us with the lovely little pink **DESERT ANEMONE** *(Anemone tuberosa),* in the buttercup family (Ranunculaceae). The underground part is tuberous, the stem or stems are four to 12 inches high, and the leaves are few, divided into three parts. The rose-colored flower is about an inch across. An inhabitant of dry, rocky slopes between 3,000 and 5,000 feet, desert anemone is found in the southwestern Colorado Desert and the eastern and northern parts of the Mojave to Utah and New Mexico. It blooms in April and May.

Desert anemone

Another desert plant that is to me altogether fanciful is **DESERT CANDLE (Caulanthus inflatus),** in the mustard family (Brassicaceae). Erect, usually unbranched, it is an annual with curiously inflated hollow stems, commonly one to two feet high, bearing numerous leaves below and many flowers above. The cluster of purplish buds at the summit of the inflated stem is particularly noticeable. The flowers have white petals and sepals that are purplish or white with purplish tips. Common on open flats and among brush below 5,000 feet from the Barstow region westward and into the San Joaquin Valley as far as Fresno County, desert candle flowers from March to May.

Another member of the mustard family is **BLUE-PODDED ROCK CRESS (Arabis glaucovalvula),** a perennial plant with a somewhat woody base, growing six to 15 inches high and more or less hoary throughout. The fuzzy sepals are about one-sixth

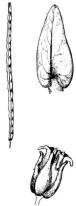

Desert candle

inch long, and the rather pink or purplish petals are slightly longer. The unusual pods are broad and flat, an inch or more long, and about one-fourth inch wide. Other species of rock cress, with narrower pods and purple or reddish flowers, may be more common. Blue-podded rock cress is found in dry, stony places between 2,500 and 5,300 feet from Bishop Creek, Inyo County, to the Eagle Mountains, Riverside County, blooming from March to May.

Blue-podded rock cress

With succulents so popular as garden and house plants, it is nice to find a member of the stonecrop family (Crassulaceae) growing wild in the desert. **PANAMINT DUDLEYA** *(Dudleya saxosa)* has a very reddish appearance, with fleshy leaves, stems, and sepals that vary from pale green to shades of bronze and red. Its petals are actually yel-low, becoming more or less red in age, and so this plant is also described in "Yellowish Flowers." Pan-amint dudleya is found in dry, stony places be-tween 3,000 and 7,000 feet in the Panamint Range and flowers in May and June. Another closely related dudleya with no common name, *D. s.* subsp. *aloides,* has practically no red on it

Panamint dudleya

and occurs on desert slopes in San Bernardino County and southward to the Laguna Mountains of eastern San Diego County. It flowers from April to June.

The pea family (Fabaceae), with its characteristic pod like that of the cultivated pea or bean, is richly represented in Califor-nia, especially by the lupines. One of these, the **ARIZONA LUPINE** *(Lupinus arizonicus),* is a rather fleshy, branched annual. The flowers are pale purplish pink, often drying violet, and are almost half-an-inch long. It is common in sandy washes and open places below 2,000 feet from eastern Inyo County southward and into Nevada and Sonora, blooming from March to May.

Also in the pea family is one of the largest of all plant genera, *Astragalus,* containing about 2,000 species, of which more than 400 occur in North America. Known under a variety of common names that include locoweed, rattleweed, and

Arizona lupine

milkvetch, this is an immense group of plants, and in California and the western states, a very complex one. **SCARLET MILKVETCH *(Astragalus coccineus)*** is one of the most vividly

Scarlet milkvetch

colored members of this huge genus. Densely hairy and almost stemless, it makes small clumps or tufts about six to 10 inches across, with silvery leaves and many bright red flowers. This gorgeous little desert plant is found in canyons and on gravelly ridges between 2,100 and 7,000 feet. Its distribution is from Owens Valley to Death Valley and southward along the edge of the deserts to northern Baja California and in Arizona.

FRECKLED MILKVETCH (Astragalus lentiginosus var. fremontii) is one of the common desert locoweeds, a perennial with loose racemes or sprays of purplish flowers. Its leaves are pinnately compound, the leaflets arranged like the parts of a feather. The seedpods are very much inflated, papery membranous, and usually mottled. Common in the Mojave Desert below 6,500 feet, freckled milkvetch ranges from the east slope of the Sierra Nevada and from the White Mountains to southern Nevada. In the Colorado Desert it is largely replaced by other varieties.

Freckled milkvetch

LAYNES' RATTLE-WEED (Astragalus layneae) is a perennial with a deep-seated root, hairy and somewhat grayish foliage, and purple-tipped flowers more than half-an-inch long. The pods are sickle shaped and one to two inches long. This plant is found in sandy places, often in large colonies, between 1,500

Laynes' rattle-weed

Dyeweed

and 5,000 feet over much of the Mojave Desert, from Twenty-nine Palms to Owens and Death Valleys. Its period of bloom is from March to May.

DYEWEED (*Psorothamnus emoryi*) is a densely branched shrub in the pea family, one to three or more feet high, covered with a feltlike wool, and sprinkled with orange glands. The leaves are divided into five to seven leaflets, the calyx is rusty hairy, and the corolla is two colored, rose to purplish and white, and about one-sixth inch long. This species grows in dry, open places below 1,000 feet from the Colorado Desert to Baja California and Sonora, blooming from March to May. It gets its common name from the fact that the flower heads can be made to yield a yellowish dye.

FAIRYDUSTER (*Calliandra eriophylla*) is a densely branched little shrub, a foot or so high, with gray pubescent twigs spreading from the base. The leaves are divided into small leaflets. The rose to reddish purple flowers are produced in dense heads on the ends of short stems, with conspicuous tufts of reddish stamens that may be almost an inch long. The seedpods are typical of the pea family, two to three inches in length, flat, and silvery pubescent with dark red margins. This handsome little shrub is found in sandy washes and gullies below 1,000 feet from Imperial and eastern San Diego Counties to Texas, Baja California, and central Mexico. The flowers appear mostly in February and March.

Fairyduster

PIMA RHATANY, or **PURPLE HEATHER,** *(Krameria erecta)* is in the only genus in the rhatany family (Krameriaceae) and is an intricately branched, thorny little shrub, a foot or so high and somewhat wider, with silky woolly young growth and red purple flowers. The leaves are linear and up to half-an-inch long; the seedpod is short and armed with spines scattered on their upper parts with barbs. Rather common in rocky and sandy places, pima rhatany occurs at mostly 2,000 to 4,000

Pima rhatany, or purple heather

feet in mountains from the Death Valley region through the eastern Mojave Desert to the Colorado Desert and beyond. The other species in the genus, white rhatany *(K. grayi)*, has the barbs at the very summit of the spines in an umbrella fashion.

CALIFORNIA FAGONIA *(Fagonia laevis)* has a fruit shaped much like that of pima rhatany, but without the spines. In the caltrop family (Zygophyllaceae), California fagonia is a low, intricately branched little plant. The flowers are purplish, up to about one-third inch long, and each leaf has three leaf-

California fagonia

lets. Common chiefly on rocky slopes below 2,000 feet, it occurs through most of the Colorado Desert and into the southern Mojave Desert, extending its range into adjacent parts.

In the geranium family (Geraniaceae) are the common, weedy plants known to us as filaree or clocks, represented here by several species introduced from the Old World. **HERON BILL** *(Erodium texanum)* is an annual native geranium found in the desert, with almost prostrate stems and three-lobed leaves. The sepals are silvery with purple veins, and the petals are purple and about half-an-inch long. Growing eastward from near Riverside, it is common in dry flats and open places below 3,000 feet from the eastern Mojave Desert to Baja California and Texas. The flowers come in spring months.

Heron bill

Turpentine-broom

TURPENTINE-BROOM *(Thamnosma montana)* is in the rue family (Rutaceae), along with citrus, and like citrus it is covered with oil-bearing glands. True to its common name, it is strong scented and rather woody, with branching, broomlike, yellowish green stems one to two feet high. The narrow leaves are shed early. The flowers are purplish, about half-an-inch long, and the capsule is two lobed. Not surprisingly, this aromatic plant was used medicinally by Native Americans to aid healing. Growing on dry slopes below 5,500 feet, turpentine-broom is distributed from Inyo to Imperial and San Diego Counties and eastward to Utah and New Mexico. The flowering season is spring.

In the spurge family (Euphorbiaceae) is **GROUND SPURGE,** or **SAND MAT,** *(Chamaesyce polycarpa),* a milky-juiced perennial that occurs in smooth or hairy forms. Ground spurge has both staminate and pistillate flowers; neither have true sepals or petals but are borne in an involucre encircled by conspicuous white petal-like appendages with maroon glands. The

Ground spurge, or sand mat

Tamarix

central pistillate flower develops into a bulbous fruit, which dangles from the involucre. The species is common on the desert floor below 3,000 feet, reaches into the coastal drainage as far north as Ventura County, and extends eastward to Nevada and Sonora. Flowers can be found during many months of the year.

TAMARIX _(Tamarix ramosissima)_ is an introduced shrub or small tree in the tamarisk family (Tamaricaceae), one of several related species that have become aggressive weeds in desert areas. It is widely established along water courses and in low alkaline places, where its deep roots lower the water table. Tamarix, also commonly called salt cedar, is loosely branched, with minute scalelike leaves and tiny whitish or pinkish flowers arranged in elongate clusters grouped in great panicles. Found in washes and near water below 4,000 feet, this species may be in flower most of the year. A number of other species have become established in the deserts and coastal areas, including the athel *(T. aphylla)*, commonly planted as a windbreak in desert valleys.

APRICOT MALLOW *(Sphaeralcea ambigua)* is a perennial with a thick, woody crown and woody lower stems that grow to be one to three feet tall. It is covered with scurfy grayish or yellowish pubescence. The flowers are grenadine to peach red, up to one-and-a-half inches long. It belongs to the globemallow family (Malvaceae) and is one of our most characteristic desert plants, being widely distributed in a variety of forms and colors and growing below 4,000 feet. It blooms from March to June.

Apricot mallow

Closely related to the apricot mallow and in the same family is **DESERT FIVE-SPOT** *(Eremalche rotundifolia)*, an erect annual up to almost two feet tall, simple or branched, and stiff hairy. The corolla tends not to open up very far but to remain globular, and one has to look inside to see the five dark spots within the rose pink to lilac flower. Found frequently, typically in washes and on mesas below 4,000 feet, this charming plant extends its

Desert five-spot

range over most of our
desert areas and into
Arizona and Nevada
and blooms from
March to May.

OCOTILLO, or **CANDLE-
WOOD,** *(Fouquieria splendens* subsp. *splendens)* is
one of the most con-
spicuous and charac-
teristic shrubs of the
desert. Its dry, stout
stems can reach 20 feet
in height and are char-
acteristically furrowed,
bearing stout, spread-
ing spines that develop
from the petioles of
the principal leaves.

Ocotillo, or candlewood

Following both spring and late summer rains, secondary leaves appear in fascicles or small bundles in the axils of these spines. The scarlet flowers are about an inch long and are very conspicuous in a wet season. There are other species but only this one genus in the ocotillo family (Fouquieriaceae). Ocotillo grows below 2,500 feet from the area east of Daggett to Texas and Baja California.

Members of the cactus family (Cactaceae) grow throughout the desert and exhibit quite a variety of forms, sizes, and colors. Among these is the cushion type of cactus, with low, thick, sometimes clustered stems. **FISHHOOK CACTUS,** or **CORKSEED CACTUS,** *(Mammillaria tetrancistra)* is a cushion cactus, less than 10 inches high, with one or occasionally more hooked spines in the center of each tubercle. The name *Mammillaria* comes from the teatlike appearance of the tubercles, and members of the genus are sometimes called nipple cactus. The flower petals of fishhook cactus have rose to lavender stripes, and the scarlet fruit, which is quite persistent, can be half-an-inch long. The species is occasional on dry slopes and well-drained places below 2,000 feet in both our deserts and also reaches into Utah and Arizona. Flowers appear in April.

Fishhook cactus, or corkseed cactus

Foxtail cactus

FOXTAIL CACTUS (Escobaria vivipara var. alversonii) has one or more short cylindrical stems, four to eight inches high, with pinwheel-like clusters of white or ashy spines. The flowers, about an inch long, are magenta with deeper red midveins and white stigmas. This cactus is found on stony slopes at between 2,000 and 5,000 feet in the Little San Bernardino, Eagle, and Chuckawalla Mountains. The flowers appear in May and June.

BEAVERTAIL CACTUS (Opuntia basilaris) has flat joints and is spineless but has wicked, long sharp hairs, or glochids, so that it cannot easily be handled. The joints are often beautifully tinted with gray, lavender, or purple. The showy flowers are clustered at the upper ends of the joints and have pink magenta to deep rose or orchid petals that are up to one-and-a-half inches long, with a velvety sheen. Beavertail

Beavertail cactus

cactus frequents dry benches and fans below 6,000 feet, extending to Arizona and Utah in the east and the interior val-

Hedgehog cactus

leys of the coastal drainage in the west. There are several varieties and growth forms, including the rare Bakersfield cactus *(O. basilaris* var. *treleasei).* Flowers typically appear from March to June.

HEDGEHOG CACTUS *(Echinocereus engelmannii)* is named for the first important cactus student of this country, Dr. George Engelmann (1809–1884), of St. Louis. The plant has one or more clustered, cylindrical stems, each with 10 to 13 ribs that form a foot-tall clump or mound. The flowers are crimson magenta to purplish or lavender and one-and-a-half to three inches long. This cactus is common on gravelly slopes and benches below 7,200 feet in both our deserts, from the White Mountains to Baja California and eastward to Utah and Sonora. It flowers in April and May.

MOUND CACTUS *(Echinocereus triglochidiatus)* has many pale green stems, up to 60 or more, which commonly form mounds. Its color and habit of growth make it one of our most noticeable cacti. The flowers, which often do not open completely when in bloom, are dull scarlet to orange or red and two to almost three inches long. This cactus grows on rocky slopes between 3,000 and 7,000 feet from the San Bernardino Mountains to the White and Clark Mountains and eastward, flowering from April to June.

Mound cactus

In the carrot family (Apiaceae) is a characteristic desert plant, **LOMATIUM,** or **DESERT-PARSLEY,** *(Lomatium mohavense),* an almost stemless hoary-pubescent perennial. The leaves are finely divided with crowded segments, the flowers are small, mostly purplish, and the fruits are flattened, with a wing on either edge. It is fairly abundant on dry plains at 2,000 to 6,000 feet along the western edge of the Colorado Desert and in the Mojave northwest to Mount Pinos, Independence, and Death Valley. It flowers in April and May.

Sand food

When crossing the sand dunes between Yuma and Imperial Valley, it is a great temptation to get out of the car and wander about. The person who does so may occasionally find on the surface of the sand a woolly mass, two to five inches wide, embedded with purplish flowers and attached to a fleshy elongate underground stem. This is SAND FOOD *(Pholisma sonorae),* in the lennoa family (Lennoaceae). At one time when this plant was more abundant the fleshy parts were an important food for the local Native Americans; it is now threatened by off-road vehicle use. Sand food is a parasite on the roots of other plants. It is found on dunes and sandy areas below 1,000 feet in the eastern part of the Sonor-

Canchalagua

an Desert into Arizona and Mexico and is in bloom during April and May.

Gentians are not common in the deserts, but one member of the gentian family (Gentianaceae), **CANCHALAGUA (Centaurium venustum)**, is found along the western edge of the Mojave Desert. It is a low, pink-flowered annual, with red spots in a white throat and unusual twisted anthers. Canchalagua is widely distributed throughout California; in the western Mojave it is more common in the valleys and on slopes draining toward the coast. Flowers appear from May through July.

DESERT CALICO (Loeseliastrum matthewsii) is a member of a family well represented in the West, the phlox family (Polemoniaceae). Low, branched, and tufted, it has leaves an inch or so long with bristle-tipped teeth. The corolla is two lipped, mostly pinkish, and marked with a red-and-white pattern. Only a few inches high, this spring annual often occurs in such masses and persists for so long a time that it colors the sandy floor of the desert with pinkish patches after most

Desert calico

spring annuals are out of bloom. It is common in sandy and gravelly flats below 5,000 feet in the deserts from Inyo to Imperial Counties and to Nevada and Sonora. The flowers appear from April to June.

Also in the phlox family is **SCARLET GILIA,** or **SKY-ROCKET,** *(Ipomopsis arizonica),* a biennial or short-lived perennial that grows up to a foot high. The leaves are short and dissected, and the tubular flowers are bright red, about one inch long, and arranged in a narrow, crowded panicle. This handsome plant is found

Scarlet gilia, or skyrocket

in dry washes and rocky places mostly between 4,500 and 10,500 feet, in the Providence, New York, and Inyo Mountains, Clark Mountain, the Panamint Range, and into Utah and Arizona. Flowers may be found from May to October.

Quite different from the previous species but in the same family is **SLENDER-LEAVED IPOMOPSIS** *(Ipomopsis tenuifolia),* a many-stemmed perennial growing from a woody base, reaching about one foot high. The linear leaves may be entire or dissected. The bell-shaped flowers are about one inch long, solitary in the upper leaf axils, and scarlet with white mottling on the lobes. Slender-leaved ipomopsis is rare in California, is found on gravelly or rocky slopes and canyons from 300 to 3,500 feet, and ranges from southeastern San Diego County around Campo and Jacumba into northern Baja California. Its flowers appear from March to May.

Slender-leaved ipomopsis

True phlox can be distinguished from most other members of its family by the unequal placement of the stamens in the corolla tube. **STANSBURY'S PHLOX** *(Phlox stansburyi)* grows to less than one foot high from a branched root crown and has narrow leaves about one inch long. The flowers are rather few,

Stansbury's phlox

in open terminal clusters, about an inch long, and rose to whitish. Stansbury's phlox grows on dry, gravelly slopes and washes from 5,000 to 9,000 feet from the eastern slope of the Sierra Nevada in Mono and Inyo Counties, through the White and Inyo Mountains, and into Nevada, Arizona, and New Mexico. Flowering is from April to June.

PURPLE MAT (*Nama demissum*), in the waterleaf family (Hydrophyllaceae), is a good name for another small, prostrate annual of dry flats and slopes. In a good year it is a floriferous plant some inches across; in a dryer year, it is but a tiny tuft. The corolla is purplish red and almost half-an-inch long. Several forms and related

Purple mat

species are found throughout most of our desert area; this species is in bloom during April and May. The peculiar seed and the scales at the base of the stamens inside the corolla are shown.

In the figwort family (Scrophulariaceae) is a characteristic group of plants familiarly known as paintbrush, an inclusive name used for a number of different plants. A representative member is **DESERT INDIAN PAINTBRUSH (Castilleja angustifolia),** an herbaceous perennial that grows a foot or more high from a woody root crown. The stems have stiff, bristly hairs, and the leaves are narrow, about one inch long. The upper bracts and calyces have bright scarlet to yellowish orange tips and give most of the color to the flower spike. This species is common on dry, brushy slopes between 2,000 and 7,000 feet from the Pinto Mountains in Riverside County northward to eastern Oregon and eastward to Wyoming, Colorado, and New Mexico. The species flowers from April to August, but only in the early season in our desert.

Desert Indian paintbrush

Purple owl's-clover

PURPLE OWL'S-CLOVER (Castilleja exserta) is another paint-brush. Its flowers are in a deep red purple spike, more intensely colored than the coastal forms of the species. The corolla is a deep velvet red and may sometimes have orange yellow on the outer third of the lower lip. Growing in masses with gilias and other annuals, this plant often presents a brilliant spectacle in spring, particularly near Adelanto and on into the Antelope Valley. Found locally and in profusion in open flats on the western Mojave Desert, between 2,000 and 3,000 feet, it blooms from March to May.

Also in the figwort family is another distinctive group, the penstemons, or beard-tongues. This large genus has five stamens, but only four are functional. Several desert species occur, and they are quite different from one another. Among the red-flowered penstemons is **EATON'S FIRECRACKER (Penstemon eatonii)**. It is a perennial with few to several stems, one to three feet tall, and thickish, glabrous leaves one to four inches

Eaton's firecracker

Utah bugler

long. This species is fairly common and widespread at elevations up to 8,000 feet on desert slopes from the San Bernardino Mountains to Utah and Nevada. The period of bloom is from March to July.

Another red penstemon is **UTAH BUGLER *(Penstemon utahensis)*,** with carmine flowers less than one inch long. It has a lower growth form than *P. eatonii*, and the flowers are narrower and glandular, not smooth as in the former. Utah bugler occurs occasionally between 4,000 and 5,500 feet in rocky places in the New York Mountains and Kingston Range and into Utah and Arizona. It flowers in April and May. A similar form with rose lavender or purplish flowers and a more open inflorescence, Owens Valley penstemon *(P. confusus* subsp. *patens)*, grows in the hills surrounding Owens Valley.

Mono penstemon

MONO PENSTEMON *(Penstemon monoensis)* grows to about one foot high and has stems covered with dense, ashy, backward-pointing hairs. The tubular-funnelform flowers are rose purple or wine red, glandular pubescent, about two-thirds of an inch long, and clustered in crowded whorls. It is found in dry, stony places at 3,800 to 6,000 feet along the base of the White and Inyo Mountains. May to June is the typical flowering time. A somewhat similar species, lime penstemon *(P. calcareus)*, has a light rose to rose purple flower and grows in the Grapevine and Providence Mountains.

Another large group in the penstemon family is the monkey-flowers, characterized by a calyx with strongly angled seg-

Bigelow's
monkeyflower

ments. One desert species is **BIGELOW'S MONKEYFLOWER** *(Mimulus bigelovii)*. It is a low, densely glandular-pubescent annual, with leaves up to one inch long. The flowers have rose to dark magenta corollas, a golden throat marked with two small dark maroon patches, and are mostly clustered near the tips of the stem branches. It is common in dry sandy or gravelly washes and canyons below 9,000 feet in the Mojave and Sonoran Deserts from Mono County southward. Mojave monkeyflower *(M. mohavensis)* is another small, glandular desert annual with a red purple, pale-margined flower and is found in the region about Barstow and Victorville.

BROOM-RAPE, or **OROBANCHE,** *(Orobanche cooperi),* in the broom-rape family (Orobanchaceae), is parasitic on the roots of other plants. The stout, fleshy stems may be single or branched and often form large clumps up to a foot in height. They contain no chlorophyll, are purplish gray, and have reduced, scalelike leaves. Purplish flowers are more than half-an-inch long. This broom-rape is largely parasitic on burro-

Broom-rape, or
orobanche

weed *(Ambrosia dumosa)* and may also damage tomatoes and
other crops in cultivated valleys. It grows throughout the
desert region in association with its host plants, in sandy flats
and washes below 1,500 feet.

DESERT-WILLOW (*Chilopsis linearis* subsp. *arcuata*), a large shrub
in the bignonia family (Bignoniaceae), is related to a number
of familiar cultivated vines with showy flowers, and to the
long-podded catalpa tree (*Catalpa* spp.). Like its relatives,
desert-willow produces large flowers that are more than an
inch long and deep lavender to whitish, with purplish lines
and markings, and hanging seedpods that can be almost a
foot long. In the Victorville-Adelanto region a more deeply
colored form is in cultivation. As its name implies, the leaves
are willowlike. Common along washes and in watercourses
below 5,000 feet, the shrub is deciduous during the colder

parts of the year and flowers between May and September.

CHUPAROSA, or **BELOPERONE,** *(Justica californica)* is our only member of the large tropical acanthus family (Acanthaceae). The Greeks used the handsome leaves of the Mediterranean species *Acanthus mollis* as the model for the decoration of the capital of the Corinthian column. Our shrub, however, is often almost leafless, one to three feet high, with gray green twigs scattered with dull scarlet tubular flowers more than an inch long. Hummingbirds

Desert-willow

visit it constantly, giving it its common name, which in Spanish has reference to sucking. Chuparosa is found along sandy watercourses below 2,500 feet from the northern and western edges of the Colorado Desert to Baja California and Sonora. It blooms from March to June.

Chuparosa, or beloperone

THREAD-STEM (Nemacladus rubescens), in the bell-flower family (Campanulaceae), is easily over-looked because its slender stems and small flowers make it exceedingly incon-spicuous against its sandy background. Often it is only by a gust of wind that one be-comes aware that something on the desert surface is moving; closer examination then reveals

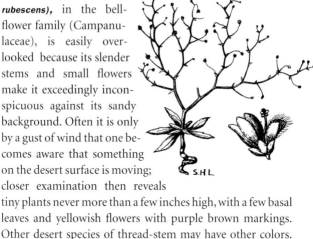

tiny plants never more than a few inches high, with a few basal leaves and yellowish flowers with purple brown markings. Other desert species of thread-stem may have other colors. Growing below 4,000 feet, this species is widely distributed throughout the deserts in California and adjacent areas and blooms mostly in April and May.

The sunflower family (Asteraceae) is the largest plant family in California and is well represented in the desert. **SALT MARSH FLEABANE (Pluchea odorata)** is an erect, green, unpleasantly scented herbaceous plant that grows up to four feet high and is branched above, with leaves two to four inches long. It has large terminal clusters of compound flower heads made up of many small pur-plish florets. Each seed or fruit bears a tuft of white hairs. The species is widely dis-tributed, found in wet places in the desert from Inyo County southward, in both freshwater and salt marshes from San Francisco and the Central Valley south-ward, and to the Atlantic Coast. It blooms from July to November.

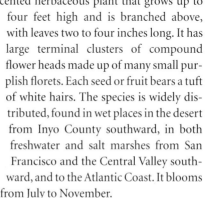

Spanish needles

SPANISH NEEDLES *(Palafoxia arida)* is a harsh herb, erect, branching, and one to two feet high, with somewhat grayish leaves and terminal heads of small pinkish white tubular florets. This common desert annual in the sunflower family grows on sandy flats and in washes below 2,500 feet and ranges as far east as Utah and northern Mexico. Flowering is from January to September. On the sand dunes east of Imperial Valley is the rare giant Spanish needle *(P. arida)*, a larger form, often perennial and woody at the base.

Also in the sunflower family is **HOLE-IN-THE-SAND,** or **NICOL-LETIA,** *(Nicolletia occidentalis),* a low perennial that grows atop a deep-seated taproot. The leaves are rather fleshy and pinnately divided into short lobes. The purplish flowers are surrounded by an involucre of bracts with evident glands (compare these to glands on dyssodia *[Adenophyllum porophyl-*

Hole-in-the-sand,
or nicolletia

loides]). Glands are also embedded on the leaf lobes, giving
the plant a strong scent. Found in shallow basins in sand from
2,500 to 4,500 feet, hole-in-the-sand ranges along the western
borders of the Mojave and Sonoran Deserts and flowers from
April to June. It is named for an early American explorer, J. N.
Nicollet.

Perhaps only a botanist would think of members of the grass family (Poaceae) as having flowers, knowing that a flower needs stamens and pistils but does not necessarily have showy sepals and petals. At any rate, in our deserts are two grasses so conspicuous and widespread that surely we want to know their names. The first of these, **BIG GALLETA** *(Pleuraphis rigida),* is a rather heavy-stemmed perennial with woody spreading rhizomes forming large, open, erect, grayish-hairy clumps two or more feet tall. The terminal spikes are two to three inches long. This grass occurs mostly in sandy places below 4,000 feet throughout our deserts and to the immediate east. It is said to be the most valuable forage grass of the desert.

Another common grass is **INDIAN RICEGRASS** *(Achnatherum hymenoides),* a densely tufted perennial with florets that are borne on filiform wiry branches in open panicles. Growing in well-drained, dry, sandy soils, Indian ricegrass ascends the

Indian ricegrass

east slopes of the Sierra Nevada and the Inyo and White Mountains to 10,000 feet and extends from our deserts to British Columbia, Manitoba, Texas, and northern Mexico. As the name implies, the native tribes gathered seeds of this plant for food, and it is quite palatable to livestock and wildlife. The flowers appear from April to July.

Although the desert may not seem a likely place for lilies, the lily family (Liliaceae) and its relatives have quite a few representatives in extremely dry parts of the earth. By means of their deeply buried bulbs, they can store water and food and remain dormant during dry times. Among these plants is the **PANAMINT MARIPOSA LILY (Calochortus panamintensis),** a simple plant with white, lilac-tinged petals and often a red or purplish-colored spot above the basal gland. It is found in dry pinyon and juniper woodland in the desert mountains between 5,000 and 9,000 feet from Inyo County northward and blooms from May to July.

Another member of the lily family is the **DESERT ZYGADENE (Zigadenus brevibracteatus),** a bulbous plant with a few basal leaves that grow to a height of almost one foot. From between the leaves grows a branching flower stalk of the same or slightly greater height. The creamy white flowers are six parted and approximately an inch across. Desert zygadene is found on open flats from the extreme northwestern Colorado Desert through the southern and western Mojave Desert and into eastern San Luis Obispo County. It flowers in April and May. (See photograph, page 72.)

Desert zygadene

DESERT LILY (Hesperocallis undulata) is one of the most out-standing of the desert wildflowers. The bulb is deep in the ground, and in a damp spring, it sends up a straight, stout, simple stem that may become several feet tall, with a flower cluster that may itself be a foot or more long. Just above the ground is a cluster of elongate blue green leaves with white margins. Each flower is white and about two inches long, with a silvery green band on the back of each petal-like segment. Desert lily is common on dry, sandy flats below 2,500 feet on the Mojave Desert from Yermo eastward and into the Colorado Desert. It blooms from March to May.

JOSHUA TREE (Yucca brevifolia) seems an unlikely member of the lily family, with its tall, branched woody habit and harsh overlapping leaves. A close look at the flowers, however, shows a typical lilylike aspect, with three outer and three inner fleshy

Desert lily

Joshua tree

petal-like segments about two inches long. Underground suckers may be sent out to start new individual plants. Joshua tree and the other yuccas are pollinated by small, white, day-flying yucca moths, which then lay their eggs in the developing fruits of the yucca. This specialized, interdependent relationship benefits both species and is described in more detail in Robert Ornduff's introduction to this book. Found on much of the Mojave Desert, Joshua tree can attain a height of 40 feet or more and blooms from March to May.

SPANISH BAYONET (*Yucca baccata*) has long, bluish green leaves edged with coarse, loose fibers and may grow to four feet tall. The individual flowers may be as much as four inches long and are tinged with red purple. They grow in a dense, heavy cluster and are followed by large, fleshy fruits, four inches or more long, that were eaten by the Native Americans. The fibers of the leaves also have economic value and have been put to a variety of uses. Spanish bayonet is found on dry slopes in the mountains of the eastern Mojave Desert between 3,000 and 4,000 feet and is more common in the states east of California. Flowers appear from April to June.

Spanish bayonet

MOJAVE YUCCA (*Yucca schidigera*) is much more common in California than Spanish bayonet (*Y. baccata*). The two species have similar long leaves with curling fibers on the margins,

Mojave yucca

but in the Mojave yucca, the leaves are mostly a yellow green and the fruit is drier and more of a capsule. The flowers are an inch to two inches long, cream or with a purplish tinge, and the trunk can be several feet high. This species is abundant on dry, rocky slopes and mesas below 7,000 feet and occurs in most of the desert eastward to Nevada and Arizona, extending into coastal valleys from San Bernardino County southward. Flowers appear in April and May.

A fourth species of yucca, commonly known as Our Lord's candle *(Y. whipplei)*, is also found in California. This plant is distributed in dry places beyond the deserts and is described in a companion volume, *California Spring Wildflowers.*

The genus *Nolina* is in the lily family and is obviously related to the yuccas, with its numerous thick elongate leaves arranged in a woody cluster or basal clump, but its flowers are much smaller and they persist long after flowering as conspic-

Beargrass

uous, dry, papery remains. The common species, **BEARGRASS
(Nolina parryi),** has saw-edged leaves, whereas the other desert
species, *N. bigelovii,* has smooth margins. The flower stalks
attain a height of several feet. Beargrass usually grows in rocky
places from the Little San Bernardino Mountains and the
Kingston Range to the western edge of the Colorado Desert
and on to the coastal slopes from Ventura County southward.
Flowering is from April to June.

CALIFORNIA FAN PALM *(Washingtonia filifera)* is in the palm family (Arecaceae) and is California's only native palm. Planted in
long rows along the sides of a road, it does not seem to me very

California
fan palm

attractive, but growing naturally in the desert, in irregularly placed clumps of various heights, it adds much to the landscape. Distributed about seeps, springs, and moist places from the southernmost Mojave Desert to Baja California and Arizona, it attains a height of perhaps 80 feet and bears long, open inflorescences with small flowers and, later, hard fruits that are sweet and taste like dates.

Perhaps no group of plants has more species in our California deserts than the buckwheat family (Polygonaceae). Many buckwheat are annuals, some are perennials, and some are even shrubs. Belonging to the same family as cultivated rhu-

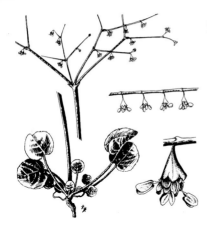

barb, they are characterized by flowers built on the plan of three, with three outer sepal-like parts and three inner petal-like ones. The color of the flower varies greatly. **FLAT-TOPPED BUCKWHEAT** (*Eriogonum deflexum*) is a good example of this family, with sometimes whitish, sometimes pink flowers. It is a wide, spreading annual with pendant flowers and is common throughout much of our California desert in washes and on adjacent slopes below 7,000 feet. This plant is usually in bloom from May to October.

CALIFORNIA BUCKWHEAT (*Eriogonum fasciculatum* var. *polifolium*) is typically a many-stemmed shrub, one to two feet tall, with numerous grayish leaves about half-an-inch long. Common on dry slopes below 7,000 feet, this buckwheat has a range that extends over both deserts into the San Joaquin Valley and inner coastal southern California and eastward to Utah. It blooms in April and May. In the extreme southern Mojave Desert and in the Eagle Mountains it is largely replaced by a low, spreading, green-leaved form, *E. f.* var. *flavoviride*.

California buckwheat

Also in the buckwheat family, with its flower built on much the same plan of three, is **SAUCER PLANT *(Oxytheca perfoliata)*.** It is a spreading annual with more or less horizontal branches up to a foot long and conspicuous fused bracts that form a series of cup-shaped disks about half-an-inch across. This species occurs in sandy or gravelly places from 2,400 to 6,000 feet from the Mojave Desert to Lassen County and into Arizona. It blooms from April into July.

JUNIPER MISTLETOE *(Phoradendron juniperinum)* is in the mistletoe family (Viscaceae). The leaves are reduced to scales, and the plant is smooth when young, with rather stout stems. It bears solitary yellow green spikes with a single joint that produces only a few flowers and white berries. In the eastern Mojave Desert this plant is found growing on Utah juniper, from which it can be distinguished by color and growth form. A

Juniper mistletoe

similar species, also with scalelike leaves but with finely hairy, grayish stems, is desert mistletoe *(P. californicum)*, a common parasite on catclaw *(Acacia greggii)*, tamarix *(Tamarix ramosissima)*, mesquite *(Prosopis glandulosa* var. *torreyana)*, palo verde *(Cercidium floridum* subsp. *floridum)*, creosote bush *(Larrea tridentata)*, and other desert shrubs. It is conspicuous with its reddish berries.

Dense mistletoe

DENSE MISTLETOE *(Phoradendron densum)* has many dense branches, closely arranged in tufts four to eight inches long. The leaves and stems are yellowish green, and the berries are straw colored. Dense mistletoe is a parasite on California juniper and is found in the western parts of the Colorado and Mojave Deserts, mostly below 5,000 feet.

In the goosefoot family (Chenopodiaceae) is the large genus familiarly known as saltbush *(Atriplex)*, which can be recognized by the pair of more or less united or fused bracts surrounding the pistillate flower and leaves that are covered with a whitish or grayish covering. This fine, scaly surface is formed of dry

Desert-holly

airsacs that grow out from the epidermal cells. These characteristics are clearly seen in **DESERT-HOLLY (Atriplex hymenelytra)**. In desert-holly the leaves are particularly conspicuous, and the whitish or even purplish appearance makes an attractive winter coating on this low, rounded shrub found in dry, alkaline places from the California deserts into Utah and Mexico. The small flowers appear in spring from January to April.

HOP-SAGE (Grayia spinosa) is a gray green shrub in the goosefoot family, often spiny and with fleshy leaves. Two bracts grow around the female flower and form a conspicuous netveined sac, almost half-an-inch long. These bracts can vary in color from white to red, so this plant is described in both sections of this book and illustrated in "Reddish Flowers." Rare in the western Colorado Desert, hop-sage is common in the Mojave Desert between 2,500 and 7,500 feet and ranges northward to Lassen and Siskiyou Counties, then to eastern Washington and to Wyoming and Arizona. The inconspicuous flowers bloom from March to June.

In this same goosefoot family of small-flowered plants is **WINTER FAT (Krascheninnikovia lanata),** a low, erect shrub with white-woolly star-shaped hairs throughout and with slender, entire leaves. Winter fat has two different kinds of flowers: a male flower with a four-lobed calyx and four stamens and a female flower with a pair of bracts surrounding a pistil. The flowers are so numerous that they make great tufts with silvery or rusty hairs. This is an important forage plant and is common on flats and rocky mesas mostly above 2,000 feet. Winter fat is found from the desert to western Kern County, north on the east side of the Sierra Nevada and Cascade Range to eastern Washington, and into the Rocky Mountains and Texas. It blooms in spring.

Plants in the goosefoot family growing in salt marshes and moist alkaline flats are conspicuously fleshy. **IODINE BUSH** *(Allenrolfea occidentalis)* is a good example, with fleshy, jointed stems and minute, scalelike leaves. The flowers are borne three to five in the joint of a fleshy, flat scale, in terminal spikes. Each flower has four or five lobes, one or two stamens, and a pistil. Iodine bush grows on moist saline soils and alkali sinks throughout the deserts and into central California, and it flowers from June to August. A related genus, pickleweed *(Salicornia),* is most common in coastal salt marshes. Pickleweed has branches and flower clusters that are opposite each other, whereas in iodine bush they are alternate.

Iodine bush

RUSSIAN THISTLE, or **TUMBLEWEED,** *(Salsola tragus)* is a weed in the goosefoot family that was introduced many years ago from Eurasia and has become tremendously common in the West. In spring the young growth is fleshy and readily eaten by cattle, but as it matures its spine-

Russian thistle, or tumbleweed

tipped scalelike leaves become very sharp and its seeds develop without interference. When ripe, it rounds up, breaks loose at the root, and is whirled across the desert plains by the strong wind, scattering its seeds as it travels. Found in disturbed places, Russian thistle flowers from July through October.

Next we come to the four o'clock family (Nyctaginaceae), in which several flowers may be grouped in a involucre of showy bracts; a familiar example is the cultivated bougainvillea. Quite common in the desert is **WISHBONE BUSH,** or **FOUR O'CLOCK,** *(Mirabilis bigelovii)*. As the name indicates, the flowers open in the late after-

Wishbone bush, or four o'clock

noon. The funnel-shaped white flowers are borne several to a calyxlike involucre. Wishbone bush grows throughout the deserts in rocky places, especially canyons, below 7,000 feet, and flowers in spring (March to June) and fall (October to November).

Sand-cress, or pussypaws

In the purslane family (Portulacaceae), along with the garden plant portulaca, bitter root *(Lewisia rediviva),* and miner's-lettuce *(Claytonia perfoliata),* is the desert plant **SAND-CRESS,** or **PUSSYPAWS, (Calyptridium monandrum)**. A small fleshy annual, sand-cress has a rosette of basal leaves and spreading stems with smaller reddish leaves. The flowers are tiny, with two fleshy sepals and usually three white petals. The fleshy fruit is quite elongate and flattened and projects out of the persistent calyx. Sand-cress is common in open sandy places, sometimes on burns, below 6,000 feet from Mono County southward, extending along the west side of the San Joaquin Valley, eastward to Nevada, and southward to Sonora. It is a spring bloomer.

Onyx flower, or frost mat

The pink family (Caryophyllaceae) is familiar to everyone who knows the garden pink, carnation, and baby's breath and who recognizes weeds such as chickweed. Many of the species in this family, although small flowered, have character and charm; this is no less true on the desert. Take as an example **ONYX FLOWER,** or **FROST MAT, (Achyronychia cooperi),** a little prostrate annual that forms small greenish white mats on the ground. The minute white flowers have translucent sepals and are borne in conspicuous tufts, and there are thin, dry, silvery sepals at the base of the small leaves. This species is common below 3,000 feet on sandy flats and in washes in the Colorado and eastern Mojave Deserts and into Arizona. It flowers from January to May.

In the same family is **DESERT SANDWORT (Arenaria macradenia),** a perennial, with slender stems one-half to one foot high growing from a branched woody crown. The paired, opposite leaves are almost needle shaped, one to two inches long, and

Desert sandwort

the white flowers, about one-third inch across, are borne in an open, branched arrangement at the ends of the stems. Desert sandwort is found on rocky slopes below 7,000 feet from Riverside County northward and into Utah and flowers in May and June.

One of the most remarkable desert plants is **RIXFORD ROCK-WORT *(Scopulophila rixfordii)*.** This low perennial in the pink family arises from a dense woody root crown, covered with small tufts of wool. The erect stems, two to six inches high, carry little clusters of tiny white flowers where the paired, narrow leaves join the stem. The sepals are broad with a greenish base and whitish margin; there are no true petals, but the sterile outer stamens are elongated and look like narrow petals. Rockwort grows in

White bear poppy

crevices in limestone at 3,000 to 7,500 feet in the Owens Valley and Death Valley regions and blooms from April to July.

The poppy family (Papaveraceae) includes some attractive plants, and one of the most distinctive is **WHITE BEAR POPPY (Arctomecon merriami),** a rather stout, shaggy perennial with long whitish hairs on the leaves and sepals. It grows up to a foot to a foot-and-a-half tall; the leaves, coarsely toothed at the apex, are one to three inches long with petioles of approximately the same length. Borne on long, smooth stems, the flowers have six white petals one to one-and-a-half inches long. This is quite a conspicuous plant, but unfortunately it is rare, found only on loose rocky slopes at 3,000 to 4,500 feet in the Death Valley region and adjacent Nevada. In the same region, just over the Nevada line, is the yellow-flowered Las Vegas bear poppy *(A. californica).*

Prickly poppy

PRICKLY POPPY *(Argemone corymbosa)* is a spiny perennial with orange-colored sap and stems two to three feet tall. The leaves are lobed and prickly, and the white crinkly flowers, two to three inches in diameter, have numerous yellow stamens. As with other poppies, the petals are shed following pollination. The spiny capsule that encloses the seeds is one inch in length. This is a beautiful plant but one not easily handled because of its armature. Found in dry places between 1,400 and 3,500 feet in the Mojave Desert, prickly poppy blooms in April and May.

None of the desert annuals is more charming than the tiny poppy **WHITE CANBYA *(Canbya candida)***. This tufted, almost stemless plant is about an inch high, with narrow leaves and many small, white, pearly flowers, each with three sepals and six petals. This little flower is often locally common but very easy to overlook on the sandy floor of the desert. Growing from 2,000 to 4,000 feet from the Victorville region south-ward through the western Mojave Desert and to Walker Pass, white canbya flowers in April and May.

White canbya

The mustard family (Brassicaceae) includes plants with a sharp or peppery taste, such as radish or cabbage, and has flowers built on the plan of four. The desert is home to many members of this family; among the white-flowered ones is **DESERT ALYSSUM (Lepidium fremontii)**. A bushy, rounded perennial, almost woody at the base and growing to a height of one to two feet, it bears innumerable small, fragrant flowers that ultimately produce flattened pods about one-sixth inch long. It is common in rocky and sandy places

Desert alyssum

below 5,000 feet from northern Riverside County to Inyo County and then to Utah and Arizona. Flowering is from March to May.

Spectacle-pod

Another member of the mustard family is **SPECTACLE-POD** *(Dithyrea californica),* an annual with mostly basal, coarsely toothed leaves. Larger plants have several ascending or spreading stems, terminating in elongate racemes of white flowers, each more than half-an-inch in diameter. The seed-pods are broad and deeply notched above and below, resembling a pair of spectacles. It is a common plant of sandy places below 4,000 feet, mostly from Inyo County southward and extending into Nevada, Arizona, and Baja California. It commonly flowers from March to May.

OLIGOMERIS *(Oligomeris linifolia)* belongs to the mignonette family (Resedaceae); like the garden mignonette it has the seedpod open at the top, and the developing seeds can be seen within. The desert plant is an odd little thing, an erect annual, a few inches to a foot tall, with linear leaves. The flowers are small and greenish, with four sepals and two petals.

Oligomeris

Oligomeris is found in open, often subsaline places below 3,000 feet on the deserts and drier spots along the southern coast and is in flower most of the year.

ROCK SPIRAEA (Petrophyton caespitosum) is a prostrate woody plant in the rose family (Rosaceae). This plant roots in cracks and crevices and forms a dense mat on the surface of bare rocks. Each flower has five sepals, five white petals, about 20 stamens, and two follicles or seedpods, a floral structure that is quite typical of the rose family. Rock spiraea grows on limestone ledges and rocks at 5,000 to 9,000 feet in the mountains of the eastern and northern Mojave Desert and eastward into the Rocky Mountains, and it blooms from May to September.

Rock spiraea

Another member of the rose family is **FERN BUSH,** or **DESERT SWEET,** *(Chamaebatiaria millefolium),* an aromatic shrub that grows to six feet high. The fernlike but rather glandular leaves and rather large terminal clusters of flowers a half-inch in diameter are characteristic of this plant. Fern bush is found on dry, rocky slopes from 3,500 to 10,200 feet from the Panamint Range and Inyo and White Mountains northward along the east slope of the Sierra Nevada to Oregon and eastward into Wyoming. It blooms from June to August.

APACHE PLUME *(Fallugia paradoxa)* has leaves that are dissected into linear divisions with rolled-under margins. It resembles two other desert shrubs in the rose family, Mojave antelope bush *(Purshia tridentata* var. *glandulosa)* and Stansbury's antelope bush *(P. mexicana* var. *stansburyana)* but is distinguished from them by the numerous pistils in its white flower. The flower, about half-an-inch long, is borne on the end of a long, bare stem, and the feathery styles become an inch or longer in fruit. Apache plume grows on dry,

Apache plume

Stansbury's antelope bush

rocky slopes between 4,000 and 5,600 feet in the mountains of the eastern Mojave Desert and eastward to Nevada, Texas, and Mexico. The flowers appear in May and June.

STANSBURY'S ANTELOPE BUSH *(Purshia mexicana* var. *stansburyana)* has gland-dotted leaves and solitary cream-colored flowers at the ends of short branches. The petals are about one-third inch long, and the plumed styles are one to two inches long in fruit. Both antelope bush and Apache plume are heavily browsed by wildlife and livestock. This shrub grows on dry slopes and in canyons at 4,000 to 8,000 feet from the White Mountains to the Providence Mountains and beyond into Colorado and Mexico. It flowers from April to July.

Also in the rose family, but with smaller, petal-less flowers, is **MOUNTAIN-MAHOGANY** *(Cercocarpus intricatus)*. Two common species occur in the desert. The one shown here has linear leaves less than half-an-inch long, with the margins curled under almost to the midrib. The lower part of the flower is tubular; the upper, deciduous bowl-shaped part with five sepals falls away after flowering. The pistil eventually grows out

Mountain-mahogany

from the lower tube and persists for some time as a slender, feathery plume with a seed at the base. This species grows at 4,000 to 9,000 feet, ranges from the southern Sierra Nevada and the White Mountains to the Providence Mountains and Clark Mountain Range and into Utah and Arizona, and flowers in May. The other common species, curl-leaf mountain-mahogany *(C. ledifolius),* has broader and longer leaves and is more widely distributed.

A large group of plants in the rose family known throughout the north temperate regions are the stone fruits in the genus *Prunus.* In the desert is the **DESERT AL-MOND (Prunus fasciculata),** a much-branched deciduous shrub that may reach eight feet high. Its leaves are in bundles or fascicles; the flowers are quite small with petals about one-tenth inch long. The almond-shaped fruits are approximately one-third inch

SHL.

Desert apricot

long. Desert almond is common over much of our area, on dry slopes and in washes between 2,500 and 6,500 feet. It flowers from March to May.

DESERT APRICOT (*Prunus fremontii*) is a rigidly branched, deciduous shrub with sweet, fragrant plumlike or cherrylike blossoms that are much visited by bees. The twigs end in thorns, and the broad leaves are similar to the familiar cultivated fruit trees in the same genus. The white flower, about half-an-inch across, produces a small yellowish fruit with a large stone. Found below 4,000 feet in canyons and rocky places along the western edge of the Colorado Desert from the Palm Springs region to Baja California, desert apricot is in bloom in early spring, in February and March.

The crossosoma family (Crossosomataceae), a small family of deciduous shrubs, occurs only in southwestern North America. In California we have two species: Catalina crossosoma (*Crossosoma californium*) grows on Santa Catalina and San Clemente Islands, and **BIGELOW'S CROSSOSOMA (*Crossosoma***

Bigelow's
crossosoma

bigelovii) is found in the desert. It is a stiff, much-branched, spiny shrub, two to six feet tall, with leaves up to about half-an-inch long. The white flowers, almost an inch in diameter, are followed by one to three follicles or dry fruits, each with two to five seeds. Found in dry, rocky canyons below 3,000 feet, this crossosoma is typical of the western Colorado and southern Mojave Deserts. It blooms from February to April.

Among California's desert perennials is **NARROW-LEAVED DITAXIS (Ditaxis lanceolata),** a small, inconspicuous plant in the spurge family (Euphorbiaceae). This immense family, recognized by its small flowers and three-lobed ovaries, grows in both the Old and New Worlds and includes a host of familiar plants, such as ground spurge *(Chamaesyce polycarpa),* poinsettia, and

Purple bush

castor bean. Narrow-leaved ditaxis is low growing, a few inches to a foot high, and silvery hairy on the younger twigs and has more or less lance-shaped leaves about an inch long. The flowers are tiny, with five sepals, five hairy petals, and a hairy, three-lobed seedpod. It grows in rocky places and canyons below 2,000 feet in the Colorado Desert and blooms in spring, March to May. A related species with coarse teeth at the tips of the leaves and later flowers (April to November) is Yuma ditaxis *(D. serrata)* of the Mojave Desert.

Another member of the spurge family is **PURPLE BUSH *(Tetracoccus hallii)*,** an erect shrub about two to six feet high, with stiff branches bearing small clusters of little leaves less than half-an-inch long on short, spurlike branchlets. Male and female flowers each have four to six sepals, but no petals, and are borne on separate plants. Purple bush grows in the region between the Mojave and Colorado Deserts, ranging from the Eagle, Cottonwood, and Chuckawalla Mountains to near Needles and the Ivanpah Valley and into southwestern Arizona. It flowers from March to May.

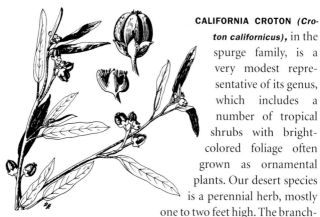

CALIFORNIA CROTON (Croton californicus), in the spurge family, is a very modest representative of its genus, which includes a number of tropical shrubs with bright-colored foliage often grown as ornamental plants. Our desert species is a perennial herb, mostly one to two feet high. The branching stems and the leaves, scarcely an inch long, are hoary or pale olive green, and the flowers are very small, without petals. In the desert California croton is found in sandy places with creosote bush and blooms from March to October.

LINEAR-LEAVED STILLINGIA (Stillingia linearifolia) is another example of the spurge family, showing the characteristic three-lobed ovary or seedpod. This is a strong-rooted perennial, a foot to two feet tall, with slender, loosely branched stems and linear leaves. Separate staminate and pistillate flowers are borne on the same plant. This plant is occasional in washes and rocky places below 3,500 feet in the deserts and sometimes in coastal areas. It flowers from March to May.

ANNUAL STILLINGIA (Stillingia spinulosa) is less than a foot high, with spreading branches and broad, toothed, three-nerved leaves. The flowers are borne in spikes, with the staminate or male flowers above and the female or pistillate ones at the

Linear-leaved stillingia

Annual stillingia

base. This nice green little annual is frequent in dry, sandy places below 3,000 feet in the Colorado and Mojave Deserts and into adjacent Nevada and Arizona. The flowers can be seen between March and May.

In the spurge family, the genus *Euphorbia* is distributed throughout the world and includes more than a thousand species, including our cultivated poinsettia. In our deserts is another representative: **BEETLE SPURGE** *(Euphorbia eriantha)* is an erect green annual, one-half to one-and-a-half feet tall, freely branched, and bears

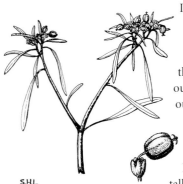

S.H.L.

Beetle spurge

narrow leaves one to two inches long. The upper green leaves form whorls around the flower clusters, as do the large red leaves of the cultivated poinsettia. Beetle spurge occurs in rocky places, such as canyons and mesas, below 3,000 feet from the Eagle Mountains and Andreas Canyon near Palm Springs to Mexico and Texas. It flowers from March to April.

JOJOBA, or **GOAT-NUT,** *(Simmondsia chinensis)* was once grouped with the cultivated box, or hedge plant, in the box family (Buxaceae) but is now placed in its own family, the jojoba family (Simmondsiaceae). It is a stiff-branched shrub, three to six feet tall, with ascending leaves and small, greenish flowers. Male and female flowers, shown in the illustration, are borne on separate plants. In addition to being a valuable forage plant, the oily, three-angled nut, almost an inch long, was used as food by the Native Americans, and a substitute for sperm whale oil can be derived from the seed wax. Jojoba is common on dry, barren slopes below 5,000 feet from the Lit-

Jojoba, or goat-nut

Lotebush

tle San Bernardino Mountains to Imperial County and westward to the inland coastal valleys. It blooms from March
to May.

LOTEBUSH *(Ziziphus parryi* **var.** *parryi)* is a desert
shrub in the buckthorn family (Rhamnaceae).
It is five to 15 feet tall, with spiny zigzag
branchlets and broad leaves about
two-thirds of an inch long. The flowers are minute, but the conspicuous
feature is the yellow, plumlike fruit
that hangs on until late summer.
Care should be taken not to confuse
this plant with the similar but larger
desert apricot *(Prunus fremontii)* of
the same region. Lotebush is local on
dry slopes and in canyons along the
western edge of the Colorado Desert

from Morongo Pass to Baja California. It blooms early in spring, February through April.

SANDPAPER PLANT is a fitting name for **Petalonyx thurberi** because its surface is covered with short barbed hairs that are rough to the touch, a characteristic of the loasa family (Loasaceae). Woody at the base, with many low, spreading, grayish stems one to two feet long, sandpaper plant has numerous sessile leaves one-fourth to one inch long. Fragrant white flowers with five sepals and five petals, arranged in terminal clusters, are much visited by bees, and sometimes the plant is called honeybush. The leaves, covered with barbed hairs, adhere to suede jackets, woolly sweaters, and socks, as many a walker has learned. Found in dry sandy or gravelly places below 4,000 feet in the Mojave and Colorado Deserts and into Nevada, Arizona, and Mexico, this plant blooms from May to June.

Sandpaper plant

Blazing star is a general name given to many different species of *Mentzelia,* another genus in the loasa family. One of the finest is **WHITE-BRACTED STICK-LEAF (Mentzelia involucrata),** an erect bushy annual about one foot high, with stout, pubescent stems and coarsely toothed leaves. The satiny petals are pale cream with reddish veins and are typically one-and-a-half to two-and-a-half inches long; plants from the northern Colorado Desert have smaller petals, less than an inch in length. Both are found on roadside embankments and in sandy, grav-

White-bracted stick-leaf

elly, or rocky places below 4,500 feet in the deserts and into Baja California and bloom from January to May.

DESERT ROCK-NETTLE (*Eucnide urens*) is a good name for a plant with stinging hairs, even though it is not related to the true nettle. This plant, like the two previous species, is in the loasa family, characterized by needlelike, rough, or stinging hairs.

Desert rock-nettle

Desert rock-nettle is a rounded bush one to two feet high, very rough with bristly hairs. The stems are straw colored, the coarsely toothed ovate leaves are one to two inches long, and the cream flowers one to one-and-a-half inches long. It grows in dry, rocky places at 2,000 to 4,500 feet from the Death Valley region to Utah and Arizona, and it flowers from April to June.

The evening-primrose family (Onagraceae) has flowers built on multiples of fours, like the mustard family, but is distinguished by the position of its ovary, or seed-bearing fruit, which is situated below the petals instead of above them. One of the best-known species is called **DEVIL'S LANTERN, LION-IN-A-CAGE,** or **BASKET EVENING-PRIMROSE,** *(Oenothera deltoides),* a coarse winter or spring annual with several recognized subspecies. The flowers open in the early evening; the stigma has four linear lobes, and the white petals are one to one-and-a-half inches long, turning pink with age. After the plant dies, the stems curl inward around the narrow structure holding

Devil's lantern, lion-in-a-cage, or basket evening-primrose

the seeds, forming an odd basket that breaks loose and tumbles about the landscape, scattering seeds. Common in sandy places below 3,500 feet, this plant, in one form or another, extends over the deserts into the San Joaquin Valley in the west, to Modoc County in the north, and to Utah, Arizona, and Baja California. Flowers come mostly from March to May.

CESPITOSE EVENING-PRIMROSE *(Oenothera caespitosa* subsp. *marginata),* also in the evening-primrose family, is a tufted or cushionlike perennial, stemless or short stemmed, more or less hairy, with narrow, lobed leaves and fragrant large flowers that open in the evening. Its short, thick, tapering fruit with little bumps or

Cespitose evening-primrose

tubercles along it distinguishes this species from the previous species, devil's lantern *(O. deltoides).* Cespitose evening-primrose is occasional on dry, mostly stony slopes between 3,000 and 10,000 feet, and its range extends from the Santa Rosa Mountains to the White Mountains and into Utah and Arizona. The typical time of bloom is April through August.

An evening-primrose family member sometimes called **BOTTLE-CLEANER *(Camissonia boothi)*** is an annual with

Bottle-cleaner

Wild honeysuckle,
or linda tarde

white flowers and a round stigma. The dried, persistent seed-pods make a cluster resembling a test-tube brush, giving this plant its common name. Found on dry, open slopes and plains below 7,000 feet, from Monterey and San Benito Counties in the west to Utah and Nevada in the east and Washington in the north, bottle-cleaner blooms from March to June. A number of subspecies vary in petal shape and the thickness of stem and capsule.

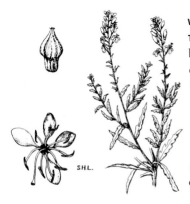

WILD HONEYSUCKLE, or **LINDA TARDE,** *(Gaura coccinea)* is a bushy perennial in the evening-primrose family, with leaves about an inch long. The white flowers are half-an-inch in diameter and turn pinkish in age, producing a hard, nutlike capsule. The species grows on dry slopes, especially on

SHL.

Twinfruit

limestone, in the mountains of the eastern Mojave. It blooms from April to June. This native desert species may become a locally abundant weed on disturbed sites outside its original habitat and range.

TWINFRUIT (*Menodora spinescens*) is a spiny little shrub in the olive family (Oleaceae). Not more than a couple of feet high, it has spreading, irregularly divergent branches bearing spines and small leaves as much as half-an-inch long. The flowers have five to seven narrow sepals about one-sixth inch long, white petals with brownish purple backs, and two-lobed capsules. Twinfruit grows on dry mesas and slopes, mostly between 3,500 and 6,500 feet from Owens Valley to the eastern Mojave Desert and into Nevada and Arizona, and is in bloom during April and May.

Amsonia

AMSONIA *(Amsonia tomentosa),* in the dogbane family (Apocyanceae), is a genus that is distributed primarily in North America and Japan. This desert species is a perennial herb, a foot or more tall, with slightly bluish flowers that soon fade to whitish. The pods are two to three or more inches long, much like those of the related species Indian hemp *(Apocynum cannabinum)* and oleander *(Nerium oleander).* Some individual plants are hairless and green leaved, and others are white woolly. Both forms are found in dry places between 2,500 and 6,000 feet from the northern edge of the Colorado Desert to the Panamint Range; they bloom from March to May.

The milkweed family (Asclepiadaceae) shares the characteristic of milky sap with the dogbane family but has distinctive flowers. **DESERT MILKWEED** *(Asclepias erosa)* is a perennial, about

Desert milkweed

Desert milkweed

Rush milkweed, or ajamete

two feet tall, with broad, paired leaves up to six inches long and round clusters of many flowers. The typical milkweed capsules or pods contain many flat seeds, each of which bears a tuft of white hairs. This milkweed is well distributed on the deserts below 5,000 feet and extends into the San Joaquin Valley, Utah, and Arizona. It blooms between May and July.

RUSH MILKWEED, or **AJAMETE,** *(Asclepias subulata),* is also in the milkweed family but is quite different from the previous species. It is almost shrubby, with many rushlike, almost leafless stems, three to five feet high. Leaves, when present, are threadlike and one to two inches long, and the greenish white flowers are about one-fourth inch long. Occasional in desert washes and sandy places below 2,000 feet, rush milkweed is found in the Colorado Desert and eastern Mojave Desert and can be found in bloom from April through December. A similar species, white-stemmed milkweed, or wax milkweed, *(A. albicans)*, has white-waxy stems and leaves that drop off early. It grows in rockier places and blooms in spring, March to May.

NUTTALL'S LINANTHUS *(Linanthus nuttalli)*, in the phlox family (Polemoniaceae), is a bushy perennial species that grows from a woody base and may have many erect stems, four to eight inches or more tall. Its leaves are half-an-inch or so long, in opposite pairs, and divided radially into five linear segments. Found in dry, rocky or brushy places at 4,000 to 12,000 feet, it is widely distributed from Humboldt and Trinity Counties to Modoc County, northward to Washington, southward along the eastern slope of the Sierra Nevada and other ranges to Baja California and Mexico, and eastward to the Rocky Mountains. Flowering is from May to August.

Nuttall's linanthus

Californians who know the outdoors are certainly acquainted with members of the waterleaf family (Hydrophyllaceae), including baby blue-eyes *(Nemophilia menziesii)* and wild-heliotrope *(Phacelia distans)*. In the same family is an inconspicuous but often common desert annual, with weak sprawling stems and smallish white flowers, sometimes called **FIESTA FLOWER** *(Pholistoma membranaceum)*. Each corolla lobe has a small, purplish, narrow spot. Usually found in shaded

Fiesta flower

places, under bushes or overhanging rocks, fiesta flower grows below 3,500 feet from Inyo County to Imperial County, then westward along the inner Coast Ranges to Contra Costa County. It blooms from March to May.

WHITE FORGET-ME-NOT, or **NEVADA CRYPTANTHA, (*Cryptantha nevadensis*)** is in the borage family (Boraginaceae), in which the flowers are borne mostly on coiled stems and the plant often has spiny prickly hairs. This species is a slender-stemmed annual, about one-and-a-half feet high, with close-lying hairs and very small, almost tubular flowers. The calyx is bristly. Many similar species are found in the desert, some with larger flowers, some with yellowish flowers, some of lower stature, some annual, and some perennial. They mostly grow in well-drained sandy or gravelly places and are spring bloomers. This species blooms from March to May.

S.H.L.

PECTOCARYA (*Pectocarya*) is a genus in the borage family represented in our area by a half-dozen or more different species. Only a few inches high, pectocarya is often conspicuous in California deserts and coastal areas because it grows in large masses, covering extensive sandy openings between bushes. The plant is usually much branched, with tiny white flowers and four spreading or divergent one-seeded nutlets in place of a seedpod. The various species are distinguished by the different ornamentation and other characteristics of the nutlets. Pectocarya blooms in spring, between February and May.

SCENTED PENSTEMON (*Penstemon palmeri* var. *palmeri*) is a tall plant in the figwort family (Scrophulariaceae), with leaves that may be sharply toothed and an inflorescence eight to 24 inches long. The abruptly inflated corolla is strongly two lipped, white or tinged with pink, lavender, or purple, with prominent colored lines extending into the throat from the lower lip. It is quite fragrant. Penstemons are sometimes called beard-tongues, and the sterile, shaggy-bearded stamen of this plant shows why. Fra-

Scented penstemon

grant penstemon is a species found in dry, rocky gullies from 4,000 to 6,000 feet in the mountains west of Death Valley and in the Kingston Range, Clark Mountain, and the Providence and New York Mountains, ranging also to Utah and Arizona. It flowers in May and June.

DESERT MONARDELLA (Monardella exilis) is an erect annual in the mint family (Lamiaceae), branched above, with lance-shaped leaves an inch or more long. Heads of white, half-inch flowers are borne at the ends of the stems, where they are sub-

Desert monardella

tended by, or sit above, a whorl of purplish, abruptly pointed, white-tipped bracts. Desert monardella grows on open flats between 2,000 and 3,500 feet in the western Mojave Desert and flowers in May and June. The mint family is well represented in California by the pennyroyal genus (*Monardella*), which includes both annuals and perennials. These native mints are not to be confused with the European pennyroyal. Most species of pennyroyal have a pleasant odor when crushed.

The nightshade family (Solanaceae) includes many plants that are of great economic importance to humans, such as potato, tomato, eggplant, bell pepper, tobacco, and petunia, as well as native plants with unremarkable but nonetheless ecologically valuable attributes. **BOX THORN,** or **PEACH THORN, (Lycium cooperi)** is a densely leafy, armed shrub, three to six feet

Box thorn, or peach thorn

high, with leaves about an inch long and greenish white tubular flowers almost half-an-inch long. The dry, greenish fruit is constricted toward its summit. Box thorn is found in dry places below 5,000 feet in both our deserts, in the upper San Joaquin Valley, and into Utah and Arizona. Flowers appear from March to May.

In the nightshade family is another **BOX THORN,** sometimes called **DESERT THORN,** *(Lycium brevipes),* a divaricately branched shrub with a flower that is white or nearly so, about one-third inch in length. The fruit is a small, bright red, round berry. This shrub occurs in washes and on hillsides below 1,500 feet along the western edge of the Colorado Desert to Baja California and to Sonora. Flowers come in March and April. Several other species of box thorn that vary in leaf shape, flower size, and color are found in our deserts.

DESERT TOBACCO *(Nicotiana obtusifolia),* another member of the nightshade family, is a mostly perennial, sticky herb found around rocky places. It is one to two-and-a-half feet tall, and

Box thorn, or desert thorn

the bases of the fairly large leaves clasp the stem. The foliage is heavy scented as it is in our other California wild tobaccos. The greenish white flowers are almost an inch long, and Native Americans smoked the dried plant. Desert tobacco grows below 4,000 feet from Mono County southward to Mexico and eastward to Texas. Flowering season is mostly from March to June.

Desert tobacco

JIMSON WEED *(Datura wrightii)* is a perennial about two feet high, with large, trumpet-shaped flowers four to eight inches in diameter. They are white, suffused with violet. Like other plants in the nightshade family the coarse leaves have a characteristic rank odor. The species grows in open places below 4,000 feet over most of southern and central California and eastward to Texas,

Jimson weed

blooming from April to October. A smaller-flowered relative found in the Colorado Desert, desert thorn-apple *(D. discolor)* (not shown), was used by the Coahuila tribe in initiation to manhood.

Island plantain

ISLAND PLANTAIN *(Plantago ovata)* is a small annual in the plantain family (Plantaginaceae), much more delicate than the big, coarse introduced plantains that are common weeds in lawns and waste places. The flower has four persistent, papery petals; the reddish yellow, shining seeds are flattened. Island plantain is found in open, sandy places below 4,500 feet from the deserts westward to the coast and eastward to Utah and Arizona. The flowering season is from January to April. A number of these small annual plantains are found in California, identified from one another by differences in their seeds.

In the gourd family (Curcurbitaceae) are many melonlike plants with fairly large, many-seeded fruits. But, as so often happens, the desert comes up with a surprise. **BRANDEGEA** *(Brandegea bigelovii)* is a vine that resembles a wild cucumber, but the fruit is a small, one-seeded, flattened structure less than half-an-inch long. The flowers are small: the male or staminate flower is barely one-twelfth inch across. Brandegea is local in washes and canyons below 2,500 feet from the southern Mojave Desert to Baja California and Arizona. It flowers from March to April.

Brandegea

The sunflower family (Asteraceae) is an unusually large one in the desert and can always be recognized by its compound flowers, which have numerous small florets arranged within an outer involucre, or whorl of bracts. Often the outer florets are modified into petal-like ray flowers, and the whole head simulates a solitary flower. Sunflowers and daisies are familiar examples.

BURROBUSH *(Hymenoclea salsola)* belongs to the sunflower family but has reduced heads that are not typical. It is a shrub with narrow, resinous leaves, one to two inches long, with male and female flowers in separate heads on the same plant. Each female or pistillate head has one floret surrounded by a papery involucre and looks more like cheeseweed in the mallow family than like a sunflower family member. The staminate or male flowers grow above the pistillate head. Burrobush is common in sandy washes and rocky places below 6,000 feet and is widespread over the desert and into dryer parts to the west, including the upper part of the San Joaquin Valley. It is in flower from March through June.

Burrobush

BUGSEED *(Dicoria canescens),* also in the sunflower family, is an annual, one to three feet high, with entire or toothed leaves and whitish, grayish, coarse hairs. The flower heads are many and small at the time they open. The male flowers remain small, but in the female flower the bracts or phyllaries that support one or two flowers become thin and enlarged. The illustration shows two female flowers flanking the central cluster of male flowers. Bugseed is most conspicuous in midwinter when it flowers and can be found in sandy places along roadsides and open places. A variety of forms occur in both the Mojave and Colorado Deserts and to the east of California. Flowering is from September to January.

Bugseed

WHITE LAYIA *(Layia glandulosa)* is a glandular annual in the sunflower family, one to two feet high with heads that are an inch or more across. White layia is common in sandy soils below 7,000 feet over much of our desert and into the coastal drainage area, northward to Contra Costa County, and southward to Baja California. It also ranges to eastern Washington, Idaho, and Utah, blooming from March to June.

White layia

Desert pincushion

Desert star

DESERT PINCUSHION (Chaenactis fremontii) is a good name for this green, erect annual that may grow up to a foot. The leaves are rather fleshy, often with linear lobes. The heads are pincushion-like, and the outer florets on the disk are somewhat enlarged. Each floret produces a fruit or seed with terminal papery scales. Desert pincushion is common on sandy mesas and open slopes below 3,500 feet in both the Mojave and Colorado Deserts and extends along the edges of the San Joaquin Valley to the Kettleman Hills. It flowers from March to May. Other species have more finely divided leaves, and some have yellow flowers.

DESERT STAR (Monoptilon bellioides) is a little annual that grows flat on the desert floor. It is stiff hairy, from an inch or so to several inches in diameter. It is in the sunflower family and a typical daisy, with white or pinkish ray flowers. Abundant on sandy or stony desert plains below 3,000 feet, desert star can be found in bloom from January to September.

Desert daisy

DESERT DAISY *(Erigeron concinnus* var. *concinnus)* is a perennial with a taproot and a branched, woody root crown, or caudex. The leaves are rather harsh, up to three or four inches long, and the flowers are typical of the sunflower family. The florets are in terminal, hemispheric heads, with 50 to 100 petal-like ray florets in blue, pink, or white. Found on dry, gravelly slopes at 4,000 to 6,000 feet, this plant occurs in the mountains of the eastern Mojave Desert in Inyo and San Bernardino Counties, blooming in May and June.

MULE FAT, also called **SEEP WILLOW** and **WATER-WALLY,** *(Baccharis salicifolia),* is a willowlike shrub, six to 12 feet tall. The

Mule fat, or seep willow, or water-wally

leaves are mostly entire (that is, not toothed or lobed) and covered with a slightly gluey exudation. The small flower heads are borne in terminal clusters, and each floret produces a seedlike fruit with a tuft of hairs at the tip. Mule fat grows along washes and ditch banks below 1,500 feet, is common on coastal slopes, and extends across the desert to Utah and Arizona. Flowers can be found in most seasons.

Not many species of thistle occur in the desert, but one, **DESERT THISTLE** *(Cirsium neomexicanum),* occurs sparingly over a wide area. It is a tall, white-woolly biennial in the sunflower family, with strongly spiny leaves up to one-and-a-half feet long. The heads are about two inches broad, with a sparsely woolly, rounded involucre surrounding the very slender numerous whitish flowers. This species is found in dry, rocky places between 3,500 and 6,000 feet from the mountains of the eastern Mojave Desert to Colorado and New Mexico, and it blooms in April and May. Another thistle is Mojave thistle

Desert thistle

Desert chicory

(Cirsium mohavense), found in moist alkaline places such as those near Rosamond in Antelope Valley. The middle bracts of its involucre have a conspicuous sticky ridge, and it blooms later, from July to October.

DESERT CHICORY (Rafinesquia neomexicana) is a rather weak-stemmed annual in the sunflower family, with white ray flowers that are veined rose purple on the outer side. The heads are rather large and very fragrant. A closely related species, California chicory *(R. californica),* grows on the coastal slopes as well as in the desert, but the larger-flowered desert chicory is confined to the desert,

Tobacco-weed, or
gravel-ghost

where it is common in the shade of shrubs and in canyons, its range extending to Utah and Texas. It blooms from February to May.

Some groups in the sunflower family have only linear, strap-shaped florets in the flower head, like the common dandelion. Another striking example is **TOBACCO-WEED,** or **GRAVEL-GHOST, (Atrichoseris platyphylla),** a smooth annual with fleshy, some-times spotted leaves in a rosette flat on the ground and an erect leafless stem one to several feet tall. At the summit are spreading heads of pure white flowers that are very pleasantly fragrant. Tobacco-weed is common in sandy washes in the more eastern parts of both deserts as far north as Death Valley and ranges beyond our borders to Utah and Arizona. The flowers appear from March to May.

Another member of the dandelion-like group in the sun-flower family is **TACKSTEM (Calycoseris wrightii).** This annual

Tackstem

can be distinguished from most other similar plants on the desert by the tack-shaped glands on the upper stem and other parts of the plant. The leaves are pinnately divided into short linear lobes, although the uppermost may be entire. The ray flowers are white with rose or purplish dots or streaks on the back and may be almost an inch long. Tackstem is occasional from Death Valley to the eastern Mojave Desert and the western edge of the Colorado Desert. A similar species with tack-shaped glands but with yellow flowers is not surprisingly called yellow tackstem *(C. parryi)*. Both species bloom in spring.

Blue dicks, or desert-hyacinth

BLUE DICKS, or **DESERT-HYACINTH,** *(Dichelostemma capitatum* **subsp.** *pauciflorum)* is a bulbous plant in the lily family (Lili-aceae). It has basal leaves that can be a foot or more long and sparse terminal clusters of pale blue flowers borne on slender, naked stalks one to two feet high. It grows in dry, open places over the California deserts, blooming from March to May. On coastal slopes is a darker blue form, typical of the species, which has more flowers in each cluster.

The buttercup family (Ranunculaceae) includes many familiar plants, such as larkspur, anemone, columbine, and, of course, buttercup. Although the family is more common in moister habitats, it does appear on the desert. **PARISH'S LARKSPUR** *(Delphinium parishii)* has various color forms, ranging from a typical light blue found from

Parish's larkspur

the Mojave Desert to Coachella Valley, to a deeper blue typical of the area from the Santa Rosa Mountains to Baja California, to a pinkish purple that occurs in the Mount Pinos region. Parish's larkspur grows in desert scrub habitats on slopes up to 7,500 feet and flowers from March to June.

In the pea family (Fabaceae) are a number of more or less woody plants with stems, leaves, and calyces dotted with orange glands. One of these is **SMOKE TREE (*Psorothamnus spinosus*),** an intricate mass of slender thorny branches

Parish's larkspur

covered with fine, ashy gray hairs. Smoke tree grows to a height of three to 20 feet, and the leaves fall early in the season; from a distance the plant then looks like puffs of smoke. It is common in sandy washes below 1,500 feet east and south of Daggett, ranging into Arizona and Sonora. The bright blue purple pea-shaped flowers appear in June and July after the leaves fall off. (See photograph, page 130.)

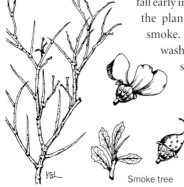

Smoke tree

Smoke tree

Indigo bush

Also in the pea family is another semiwoody plant with conspicuous orange glands, especially on the calyx, known as **INDIGO BUSH** *(Psorothamnus fremontii var. fremontii)*. An intricately branched shrub that may be six feet tall, it has grayish younger growth and dark purple blue flowers. It varies in hairiness and in the shape of its leaflets and is distributed on dry slopes below 5,000 feet from Owens and Death Valleys to Riverside County and east. The flowers come in spring, from April to May.

Another plant in the pea family with glandular foliage is **INDIAN BREADROOT** *(Pediomelum castoreum)*. This desert species is an almost stemless perennial with close-growing hairs, trifoliate leaves, and headlike clusters of blue flowers almost half-an-inch long. The starchy taproots were eaten by the local Native Americans. Indian breadroot is found on sandy flats and washes at 1,500 to 3,000 feet in the Mojave Desert from Victorville to Yermo and on to Utah and Arizona. The flowers appear in April and May.

IRONWOOD *(Olneya tesota)* is another representative of the pea family and one of the largest plants in our desert. Named for the hardness of its wood, the parched seeds of this tree were eaten by Native Americans. Mature ironwoods are spinose trees from 15 to 25 feet high, with compound leaves forming broad, grayish crowns. When the tree blooms it is covered with a profusion of violet purple flowers, almost half-an-inch long. The species is found in desert washes and on sandy fans below 2,000 feet. It ranges from the Colorado Desert into Arizona, Sonora, and Baja California, flowering late in spring. (See photograph, page 132.)

Ironwood

CATCHFLY GENTIAN *(Eustoma exaltatum),* in the gentian family (Gentianaceae), is not a typical desert species, but it is a con-

Catchfly gentian

spicuous plant about which one might well be curious. Occurring in moist places such as Thousand Palms, the Palm Springs region, and San Felipe, it is one to two feet tall, herbaceous, and smooth, with clasping upper leaves two to three inches long. The deep blue or blue lavender corolla is an inch or more long.

Broad-flowered gilia

Catchfly gentian grows along roadsides and streams and in alkaline marshes and other wet, open spots and is distributed from the desert to coastal California, Florida, and Mexico. It is in flower most of the year.

The phlox family (Polemoneaceae) is represented by **BROAD-FLOWERED GILIA *(Gilia latiflora)*,** an erect annual with a cobwebby basal rosette of leaves that are larger than those that clasp the stems. The flowers may vary from half-an-inch to an inch long, with a slender purple tube, a full throat that may be yellow or white to violet, and white to violet corolla lobes. Occurring in great masses, they make a showy display and add greatly to the color on the deserts in a good year. A number of forms of the species occur, the typical one being found on sandy flats and washes at 2,100 to 3,600 feet from inner San Luis Obispo and Santa Barbara Counties to the southwestern Mojave Desert. This plant flowers in April and May.

SLENDER-FLOWERED GILIA *(Gilia cana* subsp. *triceps),* also in the phlox family, has basal leaves that are much lobed or toothed and cobwebby, with stems to about one foot high, and an open, loose inflorescence. The corolla is from one-third to almost an inch long, with a slender tube expanding into a conical throat. The tube is more or less purplish, and the lobes are pinkish violet. This form of the species, which is quite polymorphous, occurs on dry slopes and washes at

Slender-flowered gilia

2,800 to 5,200 feet from Barstow and Kelso to the Panamint Range and White Mountains. It flowers in April and May.

BRISTLY LANGLOISIA *(Langloisia setosissima* subsp. *setosissima),* a relative of the gilia in the phlox family, is a low-growing tufted annual with short, erect or prostrate stems. The leaves, less than an inch long, are toothed, especially toward the tip. The flowers are light violet, unmarked or with purple lines, and about half-an-inch long. Bristly langloisia is found in dry, sandy places below 3,500 feet eastward and southward to Idaho, Utah, and Sonora, and it flowers from April to June.

Bristly langloisia

LILAC SUNBONNET *(Lang-loisa setosissima* subsp. *punctata)* is also in the phlox family and very similar in distribution and appearance to the previous species, except it has purple dots on the flower petals. The trumpet-shaped corolla is slightly less than an inch long, and the narrow leaves are finely bristle toothed. It is found in desert washes and dry, gravelly places mostly below 5,000 feet from

Lilac sunbonnet

the White Mountains of Inyo County southward to the San Bernardino Mountains and into Nevada and Arizona. It flowers in May and June.

A common desert annual is **DESERT ERIASTRUM** *(Eriastrum eremicum* **subsp.** *eremicum),* a more or less woolly plant that may be erect or spreading, a few inches to almost one foot high. The leaves are divided into linear segments that are mostly bristle tipped, and three to 20 flowers are grouped in each woolly cluster. The violet, two-lipped corollas are more than half-an-inch long. This member of the phlox family is found on both deserts in sandy places below 5,000 feet, ranging from Inyo to Imperial Counties and blooming from April to June.

WILD-HELIOTROPE *(Phacelia distans)* is an annual in the waterleaf family (Hydrophyllaceae) that grows one to three feet high. Frequently it is branched and even somewhat spreading, with characteristic fernlike leaves and coils of smallish blue or bluish flowers. It is common in fields, slopes, and canyons in the deserts and in coastal California as far north as Mendocino County and eastward to Nevada and Sonora. Wild-heliotrope flowers from March to June.

HELIOTROPE PHACELIA *(Phacelia crenulata)* is a characteristic desert representative of the waterleaf family and occurs in two or three forms over most of our desert. This is a handsome annual that can grow to one or two feet high in a good season. It has coiled, bell-shaped blue to violet flowers and is very glandular and strongly scented. The sticky glandular material is poisonous to many persons, including myself, and causes

Wild-heliotrope

Heliotrope phacelia

a dermatitis similar to that produced by poison-oak *(Toxicodendron diversilobum)*. Found throughout our area in sandy, gravelly washes and open places, mostly below 6,000 feet, heliotrope phacelia blooms from March through June.

The **WILD CANTERBURY-BELL** *(Phacelia campanularia)* is another member of the waterleaf family that produces dermatitis on many people. It is a striking desert annual, grow-

Wild Canterbury-bell

ing up to two or more feet tall, with broad leaves and deep blue flowers more than an inch long. Plants of this species from the southern and eastern Mojave Desert differ somewhat from the plants from the western Colorado Desert. Wild Canterbury-bell is found in dry, sandy and gravelly places below 5,000 feet, flowering from February to May.

YELLOW THROATS (*Phacelia fremontii*) is an annual, quite glandular on its upper parts and short hairy below, with spreading stems to almost one foot long. The bright blue to deep lavender flowers have a yellow tube and are almost half-an-inch long. Found on sandy or clayey slopes or flats below 7,000 feet, yellow throats ranges from Inyo to Riverside Counties and the Santa Rosa Mountains along the western edge of the San Joaquin Valley and eastward into Utah and Arizona. Flowers appear from March to May.

Yellow throats

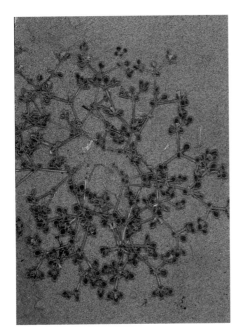

Coldenia

COLDENIA *(Tiquilia plicata)* is in the borage family (Boraginaceae). The borage family generally has its flowers in coils, like the waterleaf family, but differs in having small, hard nutlets for seeds. Coldenia is a matted perennial with prostrate stems about one foot long that grow from a deep woody root. The small, distinctive leaves have four to seven pairs of deeply impressed veins and are rather grayish hairy with close-growing hairs. The tiny flowers are one-sixth inch long and almost hidden. Growing in sandy places below 3,000 feet, coldenia is found in the Colorado Desert and the eastern Mojave Desert and in Nevada and Arizona. It flowers between April and July. Another similar species, Palmer's coldenia *(T. palmeri)*, has only two or three pairs of veins on its leaves.

Desert vervain

The vervain family (Verbenaceae) is represented in our area by **DESERT VERVAIN** *(Verbena gooddingii)*. This native perennial has several hairy stems a foot or so high, somewhat divided and lobed leaves, and headlike spikes of purplish flowers that are half-an-inch in diameter, with a tube almost as long. Found in dry canyons and on slopes at 4,000 to 6,500 feet from the eastern Mojave Desert to Utah and Arizona, this species blooms from April to June. Most of our California verbenas are introduced weeds, and this very handsome native is a pleasing contrast.

When I first came to California I was impressed by the many different species of sage or salvia I found. One of these representatives of the mint family (Lamiaceae) is the aromatic **MOJAVE SAGE** *(Salvia mohavensis),* a compact, many-branched

Mojave sage

shrub, one to more than two feet tall. The leaves, almost an inch long, have deeply furrowed veins; the flowers are pale blue or lavender and more than an inch long. Mojave sage grows in dry, rocky washes and canyons from 1,000 to 5,000 feet from the Little San Bernardino and Sheep Hole Mountains to the Clark Mountain Range and the Turtle Mountains and into Nevada and Sonora. It flowers from April to June. Another somewhat similar species, desert sage (*S. eremostachya*), has larger flowers that sit above purplish green instead of pale bracts. It grows south of the Santa Rosa Mountains.

Another conspicuous member of the mint family is **BLUE SAGE,** or **PURPLE SAGE, (*Salvia dorrii*),** a low much-branched shrub with grainy, downy leaves less than an inch long, broad

Blue sage, or purple sage

purplish or greenish bracts around the flower heads, and bright blue flowers about half-an-inch long. This sage occurs in a number of forms varying in leaf shape and size and grows in dry places between 2,500 and 8,000 feet from Los Angeles and San Bernardino Counties in the western Mojave Desert to Utah and Arizona, Idaho, and northern California (Lassen County). It blooms from May to July.

Thistle sage

THISTLE SAGE (Salvia carduacea), also in the mint family, is a simple, few-stemmed annual, one to two feet high, with a basal rosette of prickly leaves and sparse, open flower clusters. The flowers have a woolly calyx and a remarkable lavender corolla about an inch long, with a large, fan-shaped, fringed lower middle lobe. Vermilion or brick red anthers add to the interesting coloration. Thistle sage is frequent in sandy and gravelly flats below 4,500 feet across the western Mojave Desert to Contra Costa and Stanislaus Counties and through coastal southern California to Baja California. It flowers from March to June.

BLADDER-SAGE *(Salazaria mexicana)* exemplifies the characteristics of the mint family, which it shares with the true sages and other familiar plants such as oregano, thyme, horehound, and, naturally, mint: strongly aromatic qualities, opposite paired leaves, square stems, strongly two-lipped flowers, and nutlets instead of seedpods. Bladder sage is a low, intricately branched shrub with small, grayish, lance-shaped leaves about half-an-inch long. The purplish blue corolla of about the same length has dark lips and pale throat, and the calyx becomes inflated, colored, papery, and bladderlike in fruit. This species is common in dry washes and canyons below 5,000 feet from Inyo to Riverside Counties and east to Utah, Texas, and northern Mexico. The flowers, which appear from March to June, are followed by the greatly inflated bladdery calyces.

Bladder-sage

DESERT-LAVENDER *(Hyptis emoryi)*, also in the mint family, is an erect aromatic shrub, three to 10 feet high, with whitish, densely woolly leaves, stems, and calyces. The violet, two-

Desert-lavender

lipped flowers are about one-sixth inch long. Common in washes and canyons below 3,000 feet, desert-lavender is found in the Colorado Desert and the southern Mojave Desert into Arizona and Sonora. It blooms from January to May and is much visited by bees.

MOJAVE-ASTER *(Xylorhiza tortifolia var. tortifolia)* is a member of the sunflower family (Asteraceae). In my opinion one of the most attractive of the desert plants, it adds much to the color of rocky places. From a somewhat woody base, this robust perennial sends up a number of branches one to two feet high, with elongate, rather sharply toothed leaves. The long-stemmed flower heads may be up to two inches in diameter and may have from 40 to 60 petal-like ray flowers that can vary from blue violet to lavender to pinkish or nearly white. In the center is a cluster of compact yellow disk flowers. Mojave-aster is found in dry, rocky places between 2,000 and 5,500

Mojave-aster

feet from the northern Colorado Desert to the White Mountains of Inyo County and eastward to Utah and Arizona. Along the northern and western edges of the Colorado Desert, it is replaced by two other closely related species that also have large showy flowers. Mojave-aster blooms mostly from March to May but sometimes also flowers in fall.

DESERT FLEABANE *(Erigeron breweri* var. *covillei)* is a perennial in the sunflower family, with narrow leaves that feel harsh to the touch. It is a typical daisy, with central yellow tubular disk florets and petal-like, narrow blue ray florets around the margin of the inch-wide flower head. The plant multiplies by underground shoots as well as by seed, so it often forms patches several feet across. Desert fleabane is found on grassy or brushy slopes below about 6,000 feet from the north base of the San Bernardino Mountains to Inyo County and on the east and, less frequently, the west flanks of the Sierra Nevada. It flowers from May to August. Its scientific name commemorates Frederick V. Coville, who botanized in Death Valley in 1891.

S.H.L.

For those of us who grew up in a climate cooler than California's, it is difficult to become accustomed to plants that combine lilylike flowers and a woody base. But so it happens in our dry, warm southwestern states, where yuccas become trees and century plants send up woody stems that can be used for ridge poles in houses. California has three species of century plant, also called maguey or agave, all belonging to the genus *Agave,* discussed and illustrated below.

UTAH AGAVE *(Agave utahensis)* is one of these remarkable plants in the lily family (Liliaceae), with a basal cluster of foot-long fleshy, spinose, grayish leaves. After some years, this plant matures and sends up a slender flower stalk, five to seven feet high. The yellow flowers are an inch or more long and have outer and inner rows of three petal-like segments. Utah agave is uncommon, found on limestone in shadscale scrub and Joshua tree woodland in the eastern Mojave Desert, between 3,000 and 5,000 feet. The flowers appear in May through July; the plant blooms once, then dies. Shaw's agave *(A. shawii)* is a rare coastal species with broad, deep green leaves bearing red marginal prickles, origi-

Utah agave

nally growing from the San Diego region into Baja California and now also in cultivation. It is a winter bloomer.

Desert agave

A third species of agave, or century plant, is **DESERT AGAVE *(Agave deserti)*,** also in the lily family. This plant has grayish leaves with pale prickles and a subterranean trunk. The flower stalk has open branching and grows to 15 or more feet. The yellow flowers are one-and-a-half to two inches long and are followed by dry seedpods, one to two inches long. Desert agave can be found in washes and on dry slopes below 5,000 feet along the western edge of the Colorado Desert and sparingly in the Providence, Old Dad, Granite, and Whipple Mountains. It flowers from May to July. Native peoples here and in Mexico used century plants in many ways: they roasted the white base of the plant for food, fermented the sap from the young flower stalks, manufactured sandals and rope from the fibers, and constructed roofs from the dried flower stalks and overlapping shinglelike leaves.

DESERT MARIPOSA *(Calochortus kennedyi)*, in the lily family, is probably the most colorful of all the desert wildflowers. The stem may be only a few inches to more than a foot tall, with slightly grayish lower leaves, four to eight inches long. An individual plant may have up to six flowers, and these are brilliant vermilion to orange; the one- to two-inch-long petals often have brown purple spots near the base. This brightly colored flower is found in heavy soil of open or bushy places between 2,000 and 6,500 feet, from Inyo County to San Bernardino County. It blooms from April to June. In the more eastern parts of the Mojave Desert an orange or even a yellow-flowered type largely replaces the vermilion form.

Desert mariposa

The buckwheat family (Polygonaceae) is a large group in California, with small flowers that range widely in color. **DESERT TRUMPET (*Eriogonum inflatum*)** is a perennial with basal leaves and inflated stems that may be more than two feet tall. The very slender ultimate branches bear minute, hairy yellow flowers with three outer and three inner petal-like segments. Desert trumpet is common in gravelly and rocky places below 6,000 feet, from Mono County southward and eastward to Baja California, Arizona, and Utah. Flowers come in spring and fall.

BRITTLE SPINEFLOWER (*Chorizanthe brevicornu*) is also in the buckwheat family and, like other spineflowers, has its flowers enclosed in bracts that end in spinelike or bristlelike teeth. This small desert species is a yellowish green, brittle-stemmed annual with narrow basal leaves and minute flowers surrounded by bracts with recurved teeth. Although the actual flower is white, it is so small that the general overall effect of the plant is yellowish, and so the species is placed in

Desert trumpet

Brittle spineflower

this section. Brittle spineflower is common in dry, stony and gravelly places below 5,000 feet over most of our California deserts, blooming from March to June.

HONEY SWEET *(Tidestromia oblongifolia),* in the amaranth family (Amaranthaceae), is a white-woolly perennial with a low, broad habit, growing to about one foot high and twice as wide. It has very small, yellowish flowers with a pleasant odor that are borne in small clusters. Bracts surrounding the flowers may turn reddish late in the season. Honey sweet is found in washes and other dry, sandy places, generally below 2,000 feet, through the Colorado and eastern Mojave Deserts to Death Valley and then into Nevada and Arizona. It blooms from April to November.

Honey sweet

Desert barberry

The barberry family (Berberidaceae) is typically associated with more temperate habitats, but several species are adapted to dry conditions and occur in the desert mountains. **DESERT BARBERRY (Berberis fremontii)** has stiff stems, three to eight feet tall, and, like most barberries, has spiny harsh leaves that discourage browsing. Circle after circle of yellow petal-like parts make up the flowers; the berries are yellow to red, becoming dry and inflated. Found at 3,000 to 5,000 feet in the eastern Mojave Desert and westward to Cushenbury Springs, this barberry is perhaps not as common as the next entry, mahonia *(B. haematocarpa)*.

MAHONIA (Berberis haematocarpa), in the barberry family, is a stiff, gray green shrub with spine-toothed leaves arranged in groups of three to seven, yellow flowers about one-sixth inch long, and juicy purplish red berries about one-third inch in diameter. The Native Americans obtained a dark purple dye from the berries and

Mahonia

a deep yellow dye from the wood. Flowering in May and June, this species is found in dry, rocky places between 4,500 and 5,500 feet in the New York, Old Dad, and Granite Mountains of the eastern Mojave Desert. It ranges to Texas and northern Mexico.

CREAM CUPS (Platystemon californicus), a soft hairy annual in the poppy family (Papaveraceae), is almost one foot tall, with nodding buds and yellowish petals one-third to half-an-inch long. It is locally common in sandy places from the Cuyama Valley in the South Coast Ranges of Santa Barbara County to the western edge of the deserts and southward to Baja California. Cream cups blooms in spring.

CALIFORNIA POPPY (Eschscholzia parishii) is an annual, and, as one might expect, a member of the poppy family. Its sepals are fused into a cap that lifts off and is shed when the flower opens. The yellow petals are about an inch long, and the cap-

Cream cups

California poppy

sule is two to three inches long. This species is found on rocky slopes below 4,000 feet from the southern Mojave Desert to the Colorado Desert and blooms in March and April. Another desert species found mostly on the Mojave Desert, pygmy poppy *(E. minutiflora)*, is openly branched but has much smaller flowers. Mojave poppy *(E. glyptosperma)* is more widely distributed and more distinctive in appearance, with naked stems arising from a basal tuft of leaves; each stem ends in a solitary flower. These latter two species bloom March through May.

The mustard family (Brassicaceae) includes many plants that have foliage or seeds with a sharp, distinctive taste. Such a plant is **TANSY MUSTARD** *(Descurainia pinnata)***,** an erect, occasionally branched annual with finely dissected leaves. The numerous small, rather pale yellow flowers develop into an elongate seedpod with many small yellow to brown seeds. Not many years ago, a Native American basket containing some quarts of tansy mustard seeds was found stowed away under an over-hanging rock near Twentynine Palms, having been there apparently for many years. Tansy mustard has several named varieties and is common in gravelly and sandy places on the deserts and far beyond. Flowering is in the spring months.

Tansy mustard

WESTERN WALLFLOWER *(Erysimum capitatum)* is another member of the mustard family, with upright simple or branched stems about two feet tall. The very fragrant yellow to orange flowers develop erect, elongate pods. Western wallflower occurs in dry, stony places below 8,000 feet in the Mojave Desert and on the coastal slopes, ranging northward as far as British Columbia and Idaho. It blooms from March to July.

Western wallflower

Bladderpod, or bead pod

Another plant in the mustard family is **BLADDERPOD,** or **BEAD POD**, *(Lesquerella tenella),* an annual with slender spreading or ascending stems about one foot long. The bright yellow petals are one-fourth inch long, and the fruits are almost round. It grows in sandy places below 3,500 feet from the eastern Mojave Desert and the northeastern Colorado Desert to Utah and Arizona and flowers from March to May. A related species is *L. kingii,* a silvery-coated perennial found on dry, rocky slopes at 5,000 to 9,000 feet in the mountains of the Mojave.

One of California's early botanical explorers from the Old World was Thomas Coulter, who crossed the Colorado Desert through what is now San Diego County from the vicinity of Pala on to Mexico. In the rocky canyons along the western edge of the desert he found a plant later named for him, now called **COULTER'S LYRE POD** *(Lyrocarpa coulteri* **var.** *palmeri).* In the mustard family, this plant resembles spectaclepod *(Dithyrea californica),* but its distinctive fruits are larger and the narrow petals are tawny, not white. Coulter's lyre pod is perennial and blooms from December to April.

SHL

Prince's plume

PRINCE'S PLUME (Stanleya pinnata) grows to a height of three or four feet from a somewhat woody base and has deeply divided leaves, two to eight inches long, and elongate terminal racemes of yellow flowers. Individual flowers are about half-an-inch long and have prominent stamens and four petals, a distinguishing characteristic of the mustard family. The linear seedpod is one to three inches long. Apparently favoring the selenium-rich soils of desert washes and slopes, prince's plume grows at elevations from 1,000 to 5,000 feet from the north base of the Santa Rosa Mountains northward to Inyo County and westward to the Cuyama Valley. On the east it is found as far as North Dakota, Kansas, and Texas. Flowering is from April to September. Another species, Panamint plume *(S. elata)*, has entire, undivided leaves and grows in the Death Valley region.

Peppergrass

Bladderpod

PEPPERGRASS *(Lepidium flavum)* is an almost prostrate annual with yellow flowers and short, rounded seedpods that are typical of the mustard family. It is generally found in somewhat alkaline washes and flats below 4,500 feet from Inyo County to Imperial County and to Nevada and Baja California. Peppergrass blooms from March to May.

The caper family (Capparaceae) has flowers with four petals, like the mustard family. One of the most common desert representatives is **BLADDERPOD** *(Isomeris arborea),* a widely branched, ill-scented shrub, two to several feet high. The leaves have three leaflets, and the attractive yellow flowers are about half-an-inch long. The pods are inflated, in some forms rather narrow and some almost round. Bladderpod is common in somewhat salty places such as bluffs along the seacoast, interior valleys, and the deserts below 4,000 feet and can be found in flower most of the year.

Mojave stinkweed

Plants in the caper family usually have very ill-smelling foliage, and **MOJAVE STINKWEED** *(Cleomella obtusifolia)* is a well-named example. This diffusely branched annual often has long, rather trailing stems, petals almost one-fourth inch long, and a two-lobed capsule about as broad. It grows in alkaline flats below 4,000 feet from Inyo County to the Colorado Desert and into Nevada and Arizona. Its flowering season is long, from April to October.

Spiny caper

SPINY CAPER *(Oxystylis lutea),* not surprisingly in the caper family, is an annual with yellow stems up to three feet high. The flowers, crowded in head-like clusters, are scarcely one-twelfth inch long. Each flower produces two one-seeded nutlets. This plant grows on alkaline flats and washes at elevations below 2,000 feet from the Death Valley region to Tecopa and adjacent Nevada, flowering from March to October. The dried stems with the persistent spiny remains of the flowers are often conspicuous long after the death of the plant.

PANAMINT DUDLEYA (*Dudleya saxosa*) has small yellow flowers, but it is very reddish in overall appearance with fleshy stems, leaves, and sepals that vary from pale green to shades of bronze and red and petals that may become reddish in age, so it is described and illustrated in the "Reddish Flowers" section. This succulent plant is in the stonecrop family, grows in the Panamint Range west of Death Valley between 3,000 and 7,000 feet, and blooms in May and June. Another closely related dudleya with no common name, *D. s.* subsp. *aloides*, has practically no red on it and occurs on desert slopes in San Bernardino County and southward to the Laguna Mountains of eastern San Diego County. It flowers from April to June.

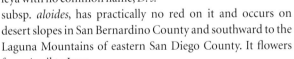

Growing in rock crevices in the desert is a representative of the rose family (Rosaceae), **ROCK IVESIA (*Ivesia saxosa*),** a small perennial with a thick, woody root and slender glandular stems. The flowers are small and light yellow and have many stamens and pistils in the center, each pistil producing a single seed. The plant grows at 3,000 to 6,000 feet along the western edge of the Colorado Desert and in the mountains of the Mojave Desert as far north as Inyo County. It flowers from April to August. (See photograph, page 162.)

Rock ivesia

Another member of the rose family is **MOJAVE ANTELOPE BUSH** *(Purshia tridentata var. glandulosa)*, a shrub with glandular twigs and leaves, the latter slightly woolly beneath. Petals are cream to yellowish, about one-fourth inch long, and the one-seeded fruit is tipped with the persistent short style. Found on dry slopes, mostly between 3,000 and 9,000 feet, from Mono County to Arizona and Baja California, Mojave antelope bush blooms from April to June.

MESQUITE, or **HONEY MESQUITE,** *(Prosopis glandulosa var. torreyana)*, a common large shrub or low tree in the pea family (Fabaceae), has crooked arched branches and compound

Antelope bush

Mesquite, or honey mesquite

leaves composed of many small, paired leaflets. The minute yellow flowers are arranged in dense spikes, two to two-and-a-half inches long, and are not very pealike. The pods are two to six inches in length. Mesquite is common in washes and low places below 5,000 feet in both the Mojave and Colorado Deserts, the upper San Joaquin Valley, the Cuyama Valley of Santa Barbara County, and other interior valleys of the coastal drainage, and eastward into Mexico. It flowers from April to June.

SCREW BEAN, or **TORNILLA,** *(Prosopis pubescens),* in the same family and genus as mesquite, is also a shrub or small tree. The foliage is somewhat grayish, with five to eight pairs of leaflets in each leaf. Small yellow flowers consisting largely of a tuft of stamens are crowded into two- or three-inch-long spikes. The outstanding feature of screw bean is the persistent coiled pod, wound into a tight springlike cylinder an inch or more long.

Found in canyons and washes below 2,500 feet from the Colorado and Mojave Deserts to western Fresno County and to Texas and Chihuahua, this plant blooms from May to July.

Screw bean, or tornilla

SPINY SENNA (Senna armata), another member of the pea family, is a rounded, many-branched shrub up to three or four feet high, with numerous yellow green stems that are leafless much of the year. The short-lived leaves have one to four pairs of leaflets. Showy flowers almost half-an-inch long are followed by yellowish, spongy pods an inch to an inch-and-a-half long. This shrub is common in sandy washes and open places below 3,700 feet over much of the desert and into Nevada and Arizona. The fragrant flowers come in April and May.

Spiny senna

Blue palo verde

The Spanish phrase "palo verde" means green tree and is an appropriate name for a number of shrubs or small trees in the pea family. Our most common California species is **BLUE PALO VERDE (Cercidium floridum)**. It has one to three pairs of tiny leaves that fall off early in the season, leaving the spiny branchlets bare most of the year. The smooth blue green bark gives the plant its color and common name. Numerous yellow flowers appear from March to May. Blue palo verde is often abun-

Catclaw

dant in washes and low, sandy places below 1,200 feet in the Colorado Desert and eastward. Another species, small-leaved palo verde (*C. microphyllum*), has four to eight pairs of leaflets and is found in the Whipple Mountains.

CATCLAW (Acacia greggii) is our only native California member of the immense genus Acacia, which is found almost universally in the dry,

Catclaw

warm parts of the world. Catclaw is a straggling deciduous shrub with short, recurved spines, leaves with four to six pairs of leaflets, and a seedpod that is typical of the pea family. The small yellow flowers, clustered in cylindrical spikes, have similar petals and many stamens. It is found in washes and canyons below 6,000 feet in the Mojave and Colorado Deserts and far beyond and blooms from April to June. Anyone who has gotten entangled in catclaw branches will agree that this name is most fitting.

Another yellow-flowered member of the pea family is **Caesalpinia virgata,** a small shrub, two to three feet high. Conspicuous and not rare, it must have a common name, but I do not know one. It has many rushlike stems with small, scattered leaves divided into numerous tiny leaflets. The stems end in long racemes of yellow to orange red flowers that are not typically pealike but that do produce flat pods up to an inch long. This plant is common in canyons and washes below 4,000 feet in the Colorado Desert and into Baja California and Sonora. It blooms from March to May.

Caesalpinia virgata

Desert deerweed,
or rock pea

DESERT DEERWEED, or **ROCK PEA,** *(Lotus rigidus)* is a member of the pea family that has truly pealike flowers, with the upper petal forming an erect banner, the two lateral petals forming wings, and the two lower forming a keel, enclosing the stamens and pistil. An erect perennial, woody at the base, desert deerweed grows one to three feet tall. The flowers are half-an-inch or more long, yellow with some red, and are borne at the ends of the stems. Common on dry slopes and in washes below 5,000 feet from Inyo County to Baja California, Arizona, and Utah, it blooms from March to May.

Probably the most dominant, widespread, and conspicuous shrub of our southwestern deserts is **CREOSOTE BUSH,** or **GREASEWOOD,** *(Larrea tridentata),* a member of the caltrop family (Zygophyllaceae). An open shrub, three to 12 feet tall, creosote bush is the dominant plant over vast areas, almost al-

Creosote bush, or greasewood

ways growing in an evenly scattered pattern. Its roots spread out not far below the surface of the soil for some distance where they can absorb what moisture is available after rains. Creosote bush clones may develop into circles or rings of plants that can be many thousands of years old. The waxy, olive green leaves consist of a pair of leaflets, and the yellow flowers have five petals, partly twisted like the vanes of a windmill. A globose, white-hairy fruit separates at maturity into five one-seeded parts. The plant is quite resinous and gives off a characteristic penetrating odor, especially after rain. This resinous sap gives it a strong flavor that discourages wildlife from browsing the plant. Creosote bush grows at elevations up to 5,000 feet and is distributed from the coastal slopes in western Riverside County through Owens Valley to southwestern Utah, southward to San Luis Potosí, eastward to beyond El Paso, into Mexico. It is even found in the deserts of Chile and Argentina. Flowering is in April and May.

Also in the caltrop family is a desert native, **CALIFORNIA KALL-STROEMIA** *(Kallstroemia californica)*, a prostrate annual that, after a rainy summer, forms mats that may carpet the desert for miles. The introduced weed commonly called puncture vine (*Tribulus terrestris*) because of the heavy spines on its five-parted fruit is a close relative and resembles this plant, but whereas California kallstroemia also has small, yellow flowers, the fruit is not spiny, merely having tubercles. This plant and a closely related species, *K. parviflora*, are found in the eastern parts of the California deserts on into Mississippi and Mexico and bloom from August to October.

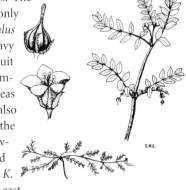

FREMONTIA, or **FLANNEL BUSH,** *(Fremontodendron californica),* in the cacao family (Sterculiaceae), is mostly a plant of the west-

Fremontia, or flannel bush

ern side, or coastal side, of the mountains, but it does occur frequently enough on the desert slopes of the western Colorado Desert and those bordering the western Mojave Desert to deserve mention here. It is a striking plant, shrubby, low to quite tall, with rounded, three-lobed leaves. It bears a profusion of yellow flowers one-and-a-half to two inches across. These desert plants are for the most part found above 3,000 feet, where spring comes late in the season, and the flowers appear largely in May and June.

CRUCIFIXION THORN *(Castela emoryi),* in the quassia or simarouba family (Simaroubaceae), is a rigid, much-branched thorny shrub, three to eight feet tall, that soon sheds its small leaves; they are rarely seen. The flowers are borne singly or in clusters on the heavy, thornlike branches and have seven or eight sepals, an equal number of petals, and five to 10 pistils that are almost separate. The shrub is occasional to rare in gravelly places and on dry plains across the southern Mojave Desert and the northern Colorado Desert to Arizona. It is in flower from June to July.

The sumac, or cashew, family (Anacardiaceae) is primarily found in warm regions. In some genera, including poison-oak *(Toxicodendron diversilobum)* and poison-ivy *(T. radicans),* the characteristic resinous or milky sap of this family may be poisonous and produce contact dermatitis.

SKUNKBUSH (Rhus trilobata)
is in the same genus with
sugarbush *(Rhus ovata)*
and lemonadeberry *(Rhus
integrifolia)* and is safe to
touch. Like lemonadeberry,
skunkbush has reddish fruits
with an acid covering. The
desert form of skunkbush is
a low shrub with three-part
leaves that have a rather
strong odor when crushed S.H.L.

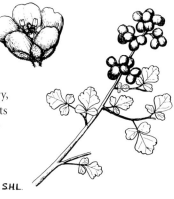

and small yellowish flowers arranged in clustered spikes. It
occurs in dry, often rocky places between 3,500 and 5,500 feet
from the mountains of the Mojave and northern Colorado
Deserts to Utah and Arizona, blooming from March to April.

FELT PLANT (Horsfordia newberryi), a
relative of hollyhock, is in the
mallow family (Malvaceae). It
is rather woody and three to
seven feet tall and has heart-
shaped felty-woolly leaves one
to three inches long. The petals
are yellow, rounded, and
one-third inch long, and the
fruit segments have wings
projecting above the calyx.
S.H.L. This plant is found in dry, rocky
places below 2,500 feet in the western
Colorado Desert to Baja California and Sonora. It flowers
from November to December and again from March to April.

SHINING STICK-LEAF (Mentzelia nitens) is in the loasa family
(Loasaceae), along with sandpaper plant *(Petalonyx thurberi).*

Shining stick-leaf

This small annual has white, shining stems, mostly lobed leaves, and barbed hairs. The flowers have many stamens and bright yellow petals that can be half-an-inch to almost an inch long. An elongated seedpod develops below the flower. Shining stick-leaf inhabits sandy and gravelly places below 5,000 feet from Mono County to River-side County and to Arizona and Utah. It is a spring bloomer.

California deserts are habitat for a good many members of the cactus family (Cactaceae). One of the most common genera in the southwestern part of the United States is *Opuntia*, recognized by its jointed

Teddy-bear cholla

stems. The joints may be cylindrical, as in the cholla group, or flattened, as in the prickly-pear group. **TEDDY-BEAR CHOLLA** *(Opuntia bigelovii)* is an erect plant, three to six feet tall. A cluster of short, lateral branches that are densely set with straw-colored spines tops the main trunk, which is covered with black spines. The flowers are yellow to pale green, more than an inch long, and set above the fruit. This species is locally common on fans and lower slopes below 3,000 feet in the Colorado Desert and the southern Mojave Desert and into Nevada and Arizona. Flowering is mostly in April.

SILVER CHOLLA, or **GOLDEN CHOLLA,** *(Opuntia echinocarpa)* is an intricately branched cactus, about two to five feet tall, covered with silvery to golden spines about an inch long. Elongated tubercles on the surfaces of the cylindrical joints are about twice as wide as they are long. Pale greenish yellow flowers have petals about an inch long. The species is found in dry, well-drained places below 6,000 feet from Mono County to Baja California, Utah, and Arizona, and it blooms from April to May.

Silver cholla, or golden cholla

Buckhorn cholla

BUCKHORN CHOLLA *(Opuntia acanthocarpa* var. *coloradensis)* is three to six feet tall and openly branched. The elongated surface tubercles on this cactus are an inch or more long and less than half as wide, and the straw-colored spines are about an inch long. Flowers are red to yellow or greenish yellow, with petals an inch to an inch-and-a-half long. Buckhorn cholla is found on dry mesas and slopes below 4,500 feet east of Twentynine Palms and Imperial Valley into Utah and Sonora. Flowers come in May and June.

MOJAVE PRICKLY-PEAR *(Opuntia erinacea* var. *erinacea)* is a low-growing cactus that forms creeping masses and has variable, flexible spines one to eight inches long. The flowers are yellow, sometimes red in age, with petals about an inch long. Occurring in various forms, Mojave prickly-pear grows on dry,

Mojave prickly-pear

Mojave tuna

gravelly and rocky slopes below 6,000 feet, ranging from the Santa Rosa Mountains to the east slope of the Sierra Nevada, the White Mountains, and eastward. It blooms mostly in May and June.

MOJAVE TUNA (*Opuntia phaeacantha*) is a prostrate cactus in the prickly-pear group, with stems up to four or five feet long, and large, flat, often erect joints about one foot long. The flat, spreading spines, about one to two inches long, red brown at base and white to yellow or yellow brown toward the tip, are grouped in clusters of one to six. The flowers are pale yellow to orange, with petals from one to two inches long. The red purple fruits are conspicuous. Found on dry slopes and in washes between 4,000 and 5,000 feet, it occurs in the eastern Mojave Desert and flowers in May and June.

Clustered barrel cactus

CLUSTERED BARREL CACTUS _(Echinocactus polycephalus var. poly-cephalus)_ has rounded or barrel-like stems about a foot thick, typically growing in clusters of 10 to 30. Each stem has about 18 to 20 ribs, each with numerous spine clusters. The yellow flowers are one to two inches long; the fruit is densely woolly. This cactus is found in well-drained places between 2,000 and 5,000 feet in the northern Colorado Desert and over much of the Mojave Desert and blooms from March to May. The closely related California barrel cactus _(Ferocactus cylindraceus)_ has taller, mostly solitary stems, and the fruits are not woolly.

The **YELLOW DESERT EVENING-PRIMROSE _(Oenothera primiveris)_,** in the evening-primrose family (Onagraceae), is a stemless winter annual with a long taproot, a rosette of basal leaves, and yellow flowers one to three inches long. The yellow petals

Yellow desert evening-primrose

open as evening approaches and age to orange red as the next day advances. It is common on the dry, rocky places of the desert, mostly below 5,000 feet, extending from the northern and eastern parts of the Colorado Desert into Inyo and Kern Counties, Utah, and Texas. Flowers appear from March to May.

Another member of the evening-primrose family is **DESERT-PRIMROSE (Camissonia brevipes)**. This plant is covered with stiff or spreading hairs, and the leaves are mostly basal. The stem terminates in a nodding tip with bright yellow flowers about an inch across, and the seed capsule is elongate and spreading. This common desert annual is found in sandy washes and on dry flats below 5,000 feet from Inyo and western San Bernardino Counties southward and

Desert-primrose

Heart-leaved-primrose

eastward to Imperial County and into Arizona and Nevada. A handsome plant, blooming from March to May, it is sometimes called yellow cups.

HEART-LEAVED-PRIMROSE (Camissonia cardiophylla), also in the evening-primrose family, is usually branched and soft hairy, one to one-and-a-half feet high, with somewhat rounded leaves. It can be an annual or a perennial. The flowers have spherical stigmas, and the petals are pale yellow, aging red, and one-third to almost one inch long. Its seedpod is on a short stalk. Heart-leaved-primrose is found in desert canyons and on mesas below 5,000 feet in the Argus and Panamint Ranges and in the Colorado Desert and into Arizona and Baja California. It is a spring bloomer.

CLAVATE-FRUITED-PRIMROSE (Camissonia claviformis), like other members of the evening-primrose family, has a spherical stigma and a club-shaped seed capsule borne on a short stalk. The small flowers are yellow to white, sometimes fading to pur-

Clavate-fruited-primrose

ple; the leaves are pinnately divided into a number of segments, and the stems are hairy. Found on rocky or sandy flats and slopes and in creosote bush scrub, common over most of the desert, this annual blooms in early spring. White-flowered varieties of clavate-fruited-primrose can be distinguished from the similar bottle-cleaner *(C. boothi)*, which has a woodier, unstalked seed capsule.

Members of the carrot family (Apiaceae) are readily recognized by their longitudinally ribbed or winged fruits and their flowers arranged in umbels, with the blossoms and seeds clustered on branches radiating from a common point. **PANAMINT INDIAN PARSNIP (Cymopterus** *panamintensis)* is a stemless heavy-rooted perennial with large tufts of finely divided leaves, small greenish yellow flowers, and fruits that are about one-third inch long. Like most members of the carrot family, it is aromatic when crushed. It grows in dry, rocky places between 2,000 and 8,000 feet in the mountains of the Mojave Desert and flowers from March to May.

TRAILING TOWNULA (*Sarcostemma hirtellum***)** has milky sap and paired leaves like other members of the milkweed family (Asclepiadaceae); it is a densely hairy, twining, slender-stemmed plant, often found climbing over other plants. The flowers are greenish yellow, about one-sixth inch long, and the slender pods are

Trailing townula

Golden gilia

an inch-and-a-half or more. Found in washes below 3,500 feet in the Colorado and eastern Mojave Deserts and adjacent Nevada and Arizona, trailing townula is in bloom from March to May. A related species, climbing milkweed *(S. cynanchoides),* is less hairy, has purplish flowers, and ranges from the desert to the coast.

Linanthus, a common genus in the phlox family (Polemoniaceae), is recognized by its paired leaves divided into linear segments. **GOLDEN GILIA *(Linanthus aureus)*** is a low-growing plant, usually several branched, with leaves at the nodes of the slender stems. The yellow flowers have an orange to brownish purple throat and are one-fourth to half-an-inch long. It is locally common over large areas in sandy places below 6,000 feet in both deserts and occasionally into the coastal valleys. Blooming is from March to June, and a white form may occur with the more usual yellow one.

DEVIL'S LETTUCE *(Amsinckia tessellata)* is in the borage family (Boraginaceae) and has the stiff prickly hairs and coiling flower clusters that are typical of that family. Flower color and size may vary within the family, but this most characteristic desert species tends to be orange and less than half an inch long. The back of the nutlet or seed has a checkered pattern, like a mosaic. Devil's lettuce is common in dry, sandy and gravelly places below 6,000 feet throughout the deserts and along the inner Coast Ranges to Contra Costa County; east of the Sierra Nevada it ranges northward to Washington. Flowers appear between March and June.

Devil's lettuce

GHOST FLOWER (Mohavea confertiflora) belongs to the same family as snapdragon and penstemon, the figwort family (Scrophulariaceae). It is a very sticky annual, simple or branched, and grows up to about one foot tall. The yellowish to white corolla is an inch or more long and closed at the throat, and the projecting part of the lower liplike petal is hairy and covered with purple dots. Only two of the stamens develop and bear pollen. The fan-

Ghost flower

shaped corolla lips and the lower petal are characteristic. Found in sandy washes and on gravelly slopes below 3,000 feet on the Mojave Desert from the Ord Mountains and Daggett eastward and southward to Nevada, Arizona, and Baja California, ghost flower blooms from March to April.

The **LESSER MOHAVEA (Mohavea breviflora),** also in the figwort family, has much the same habit of growth as ghost flower and, like it, is densely glandular, with only

Lesser mohavea

two functional stamens. The lemon yellow corolla is somewhat smaller, and the lower petal is not so conspicuously dotted. Lesser mohavea has a more limited range, found from the Death Valley region to western Nevada and northwestern Arizona. In the Mojave Desert it ranges as far south as Kelso and Bagdad. It is in bloom in March and April.

Yellow twining snapdragon

YELLOW TWINING SNAPDRAGON (Antirrhinum filipes) is a small annual in the figwort family with threadlike stems, little leaves, and yellow flowers about half-an-inch long. It climbs and twines through low bushes like a vine; both the main stems and the small stems bearing individual flowers twist and weave. Found primarily in washes and sandy places below 5,000 feet from Inyo County southward through both deserts and eastward to Utah and Nevada, this snapdragon may be found in bloom from February to May, depending on the elevation.

Calabazilla

CALABAZILLA *(Cucurbita foetidissima)* is a large, strong-smelling perennial in the gourd family (Curcurbitaceae). This amazing plant grows from an immense fusiform root and has long, trailing stems bearing erect leaves almost a foot high. The flowers are often as much as four inches long, and the female blossoms produce gourdlike striped fruits, three to four inches in diameter. Calabazilla is found in sandy and gravelly places from the San Joaquin Valley to San Diego and across the Mojave Desert to Nebraska and Texas. It flowers from June to August. Two other species of gourd or squash (*Cucurbita* spp.) occur in our area, with smaller, lobed leaves and smaller flowers.

Bedstraw is a name applied to a group of slender-stemmed plants in the madder family (Rubiaceae) with whorls of small

leaves and minute, usually four-parted, flowers. One of the most common desert species is **DESERT BEDSTRAW (Galium stellatum var. eremicum).** This bushy, much-branched plant grows one to two feet high from a woody base, has small, narrow leaves, and is covered with short hairs that are rough to the touch. The male flowers are in crowded clusters, and the female flowers that produce the small, soft-hairy fruit are at the ends of little branchlets. Common on dry, rocky slopes below 5,000 feet, desert bedstraw ranges from our deserts to Arizona and Nevada and blooms in March and April.

In the sunflower family (Asteraceae) are many yellow-flowered plants. Some have only tubular disk flowers in the flowering head, others have only strap-shaped or ray flowers; some, like the daisy, have a combination. **CALIFORNIA SPEAR-LEAVED BRICKELLBUSH (Brickellia arguta)** is a good example of a plant with only disk flowers. It is a small shrub, a foot or more tall, with multiple zigzag stems and aromatic, bright green, toothed leaves. The flower heads are about half-an-inch long and contain a number of the small yellow flowers. This brickellbush grows in rocky places below 4,500 feet from Inyo County to northern Baja California, blooming in April and May.

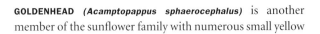

GOLDENHEAD (Acamptopappus sphaerocephalus) is another member of the sunflower family with numerous small yellow

Goldenhead

disk flowers in each head. The plant is a low, round-topped shrub, much branched, with narrow leaves about half-an-inch long and somewhat shorter rounded heads. Goldenhead grows on the open desert below 4,000 feet from Lone Pine, Inyo County, to eastern San Diego County and across the desert to Utah and Arizona. Flowering is from April to June.

SHOCKLEY GOLDENHEAD (*Acamptopappus shockleyi*) is closely related to the previous species, goldenhead (*A. sphaerocephalus*). It also is a rounded shrub, six to 18 inches high, spinescently branched and minutely rough hairy, with leaves that are about half-an-inch long. It differs from *A. sphaerocephalus*, however, in having petal-like ray flowers at the edge of its solitary flower heads. It is found on plains and washes

Shockley goldenhead

between 3,400 and 6,200 feet from the White Mountains of northern Inyo County to the Clark Mountain Range of eastern San Bernardino County and into southern Nevada. Flowers appear from April to July.

INTERIOR GOLDENBUSH *(Ericameria linearifolia)* is another close relative of goldenhead and member of the sunflower family. It is a much-branched, more or less flat-topped shrub, two to four feet tall, with crowded linear leaves about one-and-a-half inches long, covered with resinous gland dots. The compound flower heads, about an inch in diameter, include yellow ray flowers and many tubular disk flowers. It is common on dry slopes and banks below 6,000 feet from Butte and Lake Counties southward along the lower mountains, crossing the deserts into Utah and Arizona. From March to May the showy flower heads of this goldenbush add much to the interior hills of southern California. Another desert species of goldenbush, Cooper's goldenbush *(E. cooperi* var. *cooperi),* is a low, flat-topped shrub with almost linear leaves that can be half-an-

Interior goldenbush

inch long. These primary leaves are gland dotted and have fascicles of smaller leaves in their axils. The flowers are mostly tubular disk flowers, and the ray flowers are not very well developed. This is one of the common, low shrubs above 2,000 feet from the Lancaster Valley and the Little San Bernardino Mountains northward.

RABBITBRUSH *(Chrysothamnus* **spp.***)* is a commonly used name for a group of low-growing shrubs in the sunflower family found throughout the west, from the interior of California and the states about the Great Basin northward to British Columbia and eastward to South Dakota. Typically found on dry plains and slopes, often in subalkaline places, rabbit-brush can be recognized by its rayless, narrow heads borne in numerous clusters, usually narrow leaves, stems frequently covered with a very tight wool, a rather resinous odor to the foliage, and the fragrance of the yellow flowers that appear in late summer and fall. **RUBBER RABBITBRUSH *(Chrysothamnus nauseosus)*** occurs in many different forms and is found in the mountains to about 9,000 feet.

ROCK-GOLDENROD *(Petradoria pumila* subsp. *pumila)* was at one time classified with true goldenrod *(Solidago)*, a similar member of the sunflower family. Rock-goldenrod is a low, stiff plant, with resinous, light green, leafy stems. The narrow leaves are two or three inches long and have three to five longitudinal veins. The heads are few flowered, with one to three short ray flowers at the margin of a central tubular flower disk. It is found on dry limestone hillsides at 3,500 to 7,000 feet in the mountains of the eastern Mojave Desert, ranging into Wyoming and Texas. The flowers appear from July to October.

S.H.L.

SWEETBUSH *(Bebbia juncea* var. *aspera)* is a rounded shrub, two to three feet high, with many slender, brittle branches and narrow, quickly drought-deciduous leaves. Like many other plants in the sunflower family, the compound heads have only tubular disk flowers. These are very sweetly fragrant. Sweetbush is found on gravelly fans, rocky washes, and canyon sides below 4,000 feet from the White Mountains to Baja California and eastward to New Mexico. It is most common in the Colorado Desert but also occurs in interior valleys that drain to the coast. Flowers appear from April to July.

Sweetbush

The sunflower is known to all of us, but many of us do not realize that there are actually many different species. To find the desert with its quota, then, is not too surprising. One of these, sometimes called **PRAIRIE SUNFLOWER** *(Helianthus niveus* subsp. *canescens)*, is an annual that normally grows rather low but can be three feet tall or more.

Prairie sunflower

The leaves are two or three inches long and covered with stiff white hairs, giving them a grayish appearance. The flower heads, one to two inches across, include yellow ray flowers and red to dark purple disk flowers. Found in the open desert, especially in sandy places such as Borrego Valley and east of Imperial

Valley, it ranges to Texas and Mexico and blooms from March to June.

DESERT-SUNFLOWER *(Geraea canescens)* is the common name of an attractive annual, not surprisingly in the sunflower family. It is one to two feet high, glandular, and has white hairs and toothed leaves. The solitary to numerous flower heads are almost two inches across, with 10 to 20 golden rays around a yellow disk. It is common, usually growing with desert sand-verbena *(Abronia villosa)* and desert-primrose *(Camissonia brevipes)* on sandy flats below 3,000 feet in the Colorado and eastern Mojave Deserts and into Utah and Sonora. It blooms mostly from February to May and more sparingly in October and November.

Desert-sunflower

A close relative of the sunflower is **GOLDENEYE,** or **PARISH'S VIGUIERA,** *(Viguiera parishii),* a rounded subshrub one to three feet high, with many branched, harsh stems and more or less triangular leaves. The heads of yellow ray flowers are more than an inch in diameter and borne on long, naked stems.

Goldeneye is found in sandy desert canyons and on mesas below 5,000 feet in the Colorado Desert and the eastern Mojave Desert, reaching the coast near San Diego and extending its range eastward into Nevada and Arizona. It flowers from February to June and again in September and October.

S.H.L.

Goldeneye, or parish's viguiera

Also in the sunflower family and closely related to the previous species is a plant sometimes called **NEVADA SHOWY GOLDEN-EYE *(Heliomeris multiflora var. nevadensis)*.** This perennial herb has several slender erect stems and gland-dotted leaves one to two inches long. The flower heads are few, in loose clusters, and about an inch or more across. It is found in canyons at 4,000 to 7,500 feet in the mountain ranges of Inyo and northeastern San Bernardino Counties, reaching also into Utah and Arizona. It blooms from May to September.

Nevada showy golden-eye

BRITTLEBUSH, or **INCIENSO,** *(Encelia farinosa)* is another member of the sunflower family. Its woody trunk gives rise to many branches that form a compact low rounded bush, one to two-and-a-half feet high and often several feet across. The leaves are silvery gray, the flower heads are yellow or brown in the

Brittlebush, or incienso

center, and the rays are yellow. It is common about washes and on stony slopes below 3,000 feet from the Kern River Canyon and other hot interior valleys to San Diego County, over most of the California deserts, and into Utah and Sinaloa. It blooms from March to May. Other species with greener leaves occur in our deserts.

Tickseed, or Bigelow's coreopsis

Several different common species of *Coreopsis* are found in our California flora, one of which is **TICKSEED,** or **BIGELOW'S COREOPSIS,** *(Coreopsis bigelovii)*. This annual in the sunflower family has naked stems that arise from a mass of lobed leaves and varies from a few inches to almost two feet in height. It grows on dry, gravelly hillsides between 1,000 and 5,000 feet from southern Monterey and Tulare Counties southward and across much of the western Mojave Desert. It blooms from March to May. Some other annual tickseeds differ from this species only in technical features.

LEAFY-STEMMED COREOPSIS *(Coreopsis calliopsidea)* is a stout, almost fleshy

Leafy-stemmed coreopsis

annual in the sunflower family. Its leaves have narrow, linear lobes and are two to three inches long; each stem ends in a single showy, golden head, one to three inches across. It is found on dry, open, gravelly ground in the western Mojave Desert in Kern, Los Angeles, and San Bernardino Counties and into the coastal drainages from Los Angeles County to Alameda County. It flowers from March to May.

PANAMINT DAISY *(Enceliopsis covillei),* another sunflower relative, is stunning. This perennial has a stout woody taproot, big silvery leaves on long petioles, and large yellow flower heads borne on long, naked stems. The central disk may be up to two inches broad and is encircled by ray flowers that are one-and-a-half inches long. Panamint daisy is a rare plant, preferring alkaline conditions in rocky or clayey places between 1,200 and 4,000 feet on the west side of the Panamint Range. It blooms from April to June. Because one of the main threats to this lovely, scarce plant is horticultural collecting, it should be left undisturbed by anyone fortunate enough to find it in the wild. A related species, naked-stemmed daisy *(E. nudicaulis),* has smaller flowers and leaves that are less sharply pointed.

Panamint daisy

Burro-weed

One group in the sunflower family has very inconspicuous flowers, often with the male and female flowers in separate heads. The male or staminate flowers are small and tubular, and the female flowers have one to four pistils surrounded by burlike outer bracts. A good example of this group is **BURRO-WEED** *(Ambrosia dumosa)*, a low grayish subshrub one to two feet high. The leaves are divided, and the flower heads are borne on the stem tips. The burlike female heads have sharp spines and often persist for a long time. Burro-weed is one of the most common plants of the desert, often growing between plants of creosote bush. Found below 3,500 feet and ranging into Utah and Sonora, it blooms from February to June and again from September to November.

WOOLY BUR-SAGE *(Ambrosia eriocentra)* is in the same group of the sunflower family as burro-weed *(A. dumosa)* but is larger both in leaf and stature. The leaves are gray woolly, at least when young, and the male heads are situated above the woolly female ones in the inflorescence. It grows on dry slopes between 2,500 and 5,000 feet in the eastern Mojave Desert and to Utah and Arizona, flowering from March to May. (See photograph, page 198.)

S.H.L.

Woolly bur-sage

PAPER-DAISY (Psilostrophe cooperi) has an appropriate common name because its yellow ray flowers persist and become dry and papery in age. Its scientific name honors Dr. J.G. Cooper, a physiologist and ornithologist who lived from

Paper-daisy

1831 to 1902, botanized in the Mojave Desert in the 1860s, and discovered many of our desert plants. This member of the sunflower family is somewhat woody at the base, has many stems, and is white woolly throughout, especially on the younger parts. The simple undivided leaves are one to almost three inches long. Inhabiting rocky desert mesas and sandy fans between 2,000 and 5,000 feet, it is found in the eastern Mojave Desert from the Kingston and Clark Mountain Ranges to the Little San Bernardino Mountains and in the northern Colorado Desert. It responds to both spring and summer rains and in the proper year blooms twice, once in spring and once in fall.

ARIZONA HYMENOXYS *(Hymenoxys acaulis* var. *arizonica)* is a tufted perennial in the sunflower family. Its gray-silky basal leaves, one to two inches long, grow from a branched woody base. The bright yellow solitary heads are perhaps an inch across and are made up of both tubular disk flowers and marginal ray flowers. The plant is found primarily on limestone at elevations between 4,000 and 8,000 feet in the Chuckawalla, Providence, and New York Mountains and Clark Mountain Range of our eastern desert region, ranging further eastward to Colorado. It flowers from April to June. Its botanical relationships have apparently not been well understood; at various times it has been referred to eight different genera.

Arizona hymenoxys

Wallace's woolly daisy

WALLACE'S WOOLLY DAISY *(Eriophyllum wallacei)* is a very common little desert annual in the sunflower family. Persistently woolly, usually branched, it appears to grow in little tufts or mats. The leaves are three lobed at the tip, and the scattered flower heads each have five to 10 golden or yellow rays, although one form found on the western edge of the Colorado Desert may have reddish or purplish flowers. The species is common on sandy flats and fans below 5,000 feet from Mono County to Baja California, ranging eastward to Utah and Arizona. It is a spring bloomer.

ROCK-DAISY *(Perityle emoryi),* also in the sunflower family, is a low glandular annual with brittle branches and broad leaves that may be toothed or lobed. The flower heads are small, with a yellow center and whitish to yellowish rays that are not very conspicuous. Rock-daisy is common in rock crevices and among boulders below 3,000 feet through most of the desert, extending its range along the immediate coast as far north as Ventura County and to the east into Nevada and Sinaloa. Flowers appear as early as February and as late as June.

Rock-daisy

Yellowhead

YELLOWHEAD *(Trichoptilium incisum)* is another annual in the sunflower family that is loosely white woolly and aromatic. It is low and diffusely branched, with sharply toothed leaves. The yellow heads are made up of many small tubular disk flowers. Yellowhead is common on desert pavement or in sandy places below 2,200 feet in the Colorado and southern Mojave Deserts and ranges into southern Nevada, western Arizona, and northern Baja California. Flowers can be found from February to May and October to November, if the rains come at the right times.

Within the sunflower family is a small group of plants known as the desert-marigolds *(Baileya);* three species occur in California. **WILD-MARIGOLD *(Baileya multiradiata* var. *multiradiata)*** has leaves near the base of the plant and carries its large, showy heads on naked stems. The ray flowers are half-an-inch long and numerous, from 20 to 50 in each head, and the heads have a diameter of more than an inch. This attractive plant can be a biennial or a perennial and continues to bloom for many months if it has a little moisture, making it a good garden plant. It is found on sandy plains and rocky slopes from 2,000 to 5,200 feet from the eastern Mojave Desert to Utah and Texas. In the wild it flowers in spring and more sparingly in fall.

Wild-marigold

WOOLLY-MARIGOLD (Baileya pleniradiata), a close relative of the previous species, also has numerous ray flowers, but its leaves extend farther up the stems. The gray foliage and yellow heads make it an attractive plant. It is widespread in sandy places and desert roadsides below 5,000 feet. Flowers appear from March to May and October to November. A third member of the desert-marigold group, Colorado desert-marigold (B. pauciradiata), has small, pale yellow heads, each with only five to seven ray flowers, and is found in sandy soils, especially in dunes.

Woolly-marigold

Chinchweed

After summer rains the desert floor may be carpeted with a smelly little annual in the sunflower family called **CHINCH-WEED** *(Pectis papposa* var. *papposa)*. The opposite leaves are narrow, the plants are dotted with oil glands, and the yellow flowers are in small heads. Found especially on clayey and sandy flats below 5,000 feet, chinchweed ranges from the Colorado Desert to the Death Valley region and eastward to Utah, New Mexico, and northern Mexico. It was once used by the desert Native Americans for its odor and as a flavoring for cooking.

DYSSODIA *(Adenophyllum porophylloides)* is another sunflower family member with conspicuous oil glands; these are especially prominent on the bracts that surround the flower heads. It is a strong-scented perennial with a woody base and thick narrow leaves less than an inch long. The heads have orange yellow erect ray flowers that

S.H.L.

may turn purplish; sometimes these are quite lacking, and only the central tubular flowers are present. Dyssodia grows in sandy washes and on mesas and rocky slopes at below 3,500 feet from the western borders of the Colorado Desert to the southern Mojave Desert and into Arizona and Sonora. It flowers from March to June.

Dyssodia

GROUNDSEL, or **BASIN BUTTERWEED,** *(Senecio multilobatus)* is a very pretty little plant belonging to a huge group within the sunflower family. *Senecio* is one of the largest of all plant gen-

Groundsel, or basin butterweed

era, including perhaps 1,000 species. Some *Senecios* are arborescent, others are shrubby, and some are found above timberline; all are characterized by a group of bracts of equal length encircling the base of the flower head, sometimes with a few, much shorter bracts at their base. This particular species is a perennial, up to about one foot high, and the green foliage is quite without hair except for little tufts of wool in the axils of the leaves. The bright yellow heads are about an inch in diameter. It is frequently found in association with Joshua trees (*Yucca brevifolia*) and among pinyon and juniper in the mountains, on dry slopes between 4,000 and 6,500 feet in the eastern Mojave Desert and into Nevada and Arizona. It blooms from April to May.

SHRUBBY BUTTERWEED (*Senecio flaccidus* var. *monoensis*), also in the sunflower family, is more or less woody at the base, bushy, one to three feet tall, and yellowish green, with flat linear leaves sometimes dissected into narrow threadlike segments. The heads are about an inch across and clear yellow. Found on dry slopes and in washes between 2,000 and 6,500 feet, shrubby butterweed occurs in the northern Colorado Desert and in the Mojave Desert northward to Mono County. It is found as far east as Utah and Arizona, blooming from March to May and sometimes also in fall.

Shrubby butterweed

PIGMY-CEDAR (*Peucephyllum schottii*) is an aromatic shrub that can grow up to eight feet high, with terminal tufts of bright green crowded leaves up to an inch long. Like some other members of the sunflower family, the heads have no rays, just tubular central flowers that are quite yellow, although their tips may turn purplish in age. It grows in rocky places and canyons below 3,000 feet in the Colorado and eastern Mojave Deserts and in Nevada, Arizona, and northern Baja California. Flowering is from December to May. (See photograph, page 206.)

Pigmy-cedar

TURTLEBACK *(Psathyrotes ramosissima)* is a compact, round, rather flat member of the sunflower family. Covered with white wool, it has a strong turpentine-like odor, numerous thick, coarsely, and irregularly toothed leaves, and is typically an annual. The heads, about one-fourth inch high, have tubular yellow disk flowers that fade to purple. Turtleback is common on dry, hard soil of flats and ledges, largely at below 3,000 feet in both deserts, especially in the eastern part. It ranges to Utah, Arizona, and northwestern Mexico, flowering mostly from March to June but sometimes in winter.

This shrub in the sunflower family, sometimes called **CAT-CLAW HORSEBRUSH** *(Tetradymia axillaris)* is rigidly branched, densely white woolly, and three or four feet high. Its primary leaves are transformed into inch-long slender spines, and the flower heads are a clear yellow, each with a half-dozen small disk flowers. The heads are somewhat remote from one another and on separate stems. It is common on dry slopes and

Turtleback

flats at 2,000 to 6,400 feet, from the Mojave Desert northward to Mono County and eastward to Utah and Arizona. Flowers appear in spring.

Catclaw horsebrush

COTTON-THORN *(Tetradymia comosa)* is closely related to and resembles the previous species. It also is a densely white-woolly, rigidly branched bush two to four feet tall, with narrow linear leaves that may become elongated, rigid, and spinelike. The bright yellow flower heads are in small clusters at the ends of the branches. Common on dry slopes below 6,400 feet, cotton-thorn is found on the Mojave Desert as far north as Mono County and in the mountains bordering the western Colorado Desert. Other species of *Tetradymia* closely resemble these two.

TRIXIS *(Trixis californica var. californica)* is also in the sunflower family but is in a tribe or group that is much more common in the southern hemisphere than in the northern. Characteristic of this group is that each individual flower in the head has a two-lipped corolla. Trixis is a shrub about three feet high, leafy all the way up to the heads, and quite glandular. The leaves are one to two inches long, and the yellow flower heads are about half-an-inch long. It is frequent in canyons and washes below 3,000 feet and occurs in the Colorado Desert, northward in the Mojave Desert as far as the Sheep Hole Mountains, and eastward to western Texas and northern Mexico. Flowers can usually be found from February to April.

GLYPTOPLEURA, or **CARVED-SEED,** *(Glyptopleura marginata)* is a low-growing, almost stemless, dandelion-like sunflower family plant. This common species has curly lobed leaves

Glyptopleura, or carved-seed

with a whitish margin and many teeth. The flower heads are about one-and-a-half inches across and creamy yellow, and all the flowers in the head are ray-like or strap shaped. Glyptopleura is a plant of sandy flats, found at 2,000 to 3,500 feet from the western Mojave Desert into southern Utah and northwestern Arizona. It is really a charming little thing, blooming in April and May.

DESERT-DANDELION *(Malacothrix glabrata),* like the true dandelion, has a head composed entirely of strap-shaped or petal-like flowers. It is an annual in the sunflower family, usually many stemmed, each branch bearing a few heads of fragrant pale yellow flowers. The plants are quite smooth and hairless. Desert-dandelion is abundant on dry, sandy plains and washes below 6,000 feet in both deserts and sometimes in the hot interior valleys of coastal drainages from San Diego County to Santa Barbara County. Its range extends eastward into Idaho and Arizona. Flowers appear from March through June.

Desert-dandelion

Yellow saucers

Another species of *Malacothrix* is **YELLOW SAUCERS** *(Mala-cothrix sonchoides)*. It is an annual, with leaves that have callus-tipped lobes. The bright yellow heads are about an inch across. Yellow saucers is occasional in open, somewhat sandy places between 2,000 and 5,000 feet in the western and north-ern parts of the Mojave Desert, ranging northward to Modoc County and eastward to Nebraska. It blooms from April to June.

The only common name that I have found for **Anisocoma acaulis** is **SCALE BUD**. It is a low annual with a basal rosette of pinnately divided or toothed leaves that give rise to several as-cending stems, each topped with a single flower head. The cluster of bracts, or involucre, of these heads is so neat and

Scale bud

well made that it attracts attention. Each bract has reddish dots and is edged with red, producing a handsome effect. The pale yellow flowers are all strap shaped, and the head opens only in sunshine. The species is common in washes and sandy places above 2,000 feet and is found in both deserts, blooming from April to June.

GLOSSARY

Anther The pollen-bearing portion of the stamen (the male reproductive part of a plant).

Anthesis The time of blooming, during which the flower is open and functional.

Apetalous Without petals.

Appressed Pressed flat against the stem or another part of the plant.

Axil The angle formed where a leaf branch meets the stem.

Axillary In an axil.

Basal Found at or near the base of a plant.

Blade The expanded, generally flat portion of a leaf, petal, or other structure.

Boreal A term referring to plants native to high latitudes of the northern hemisphere or lower latitudes at high elevations; short for *circumboreal*.

Bract A small, leaflike or scalelike structure usually subtending a flower or cone.

Calyx The outer whorl of a flower, usually green, composed of sepals, and surrounding the petals of the corolla.

Capsule A dry, often many-seeded fruit that splits open when ripe along lines of separation or pores.

Carpel A subunit of the pistil; it may be one or many; fused or free.

Caudex The short, sometimes woody, vertical stem of a perennial plant. The plural is *caudices.*

Cauline Belonging to the stem; not basal.

Chaffy Composed of thin, dry, papery scales or bracts.

Cleft Cut or split about halfway.

Compound Composed of two or more similar parts; often used to describe leaves.

Corm A short, thick, underground bulblike stem without scales, as in crocuses or gladiolas.

Corolla Whorl of flower parts (petals) immediately inside or above the calyx.

Crenate Having a scalloped margin with shallow, rounded teeth.

Decompound Divided more than once.

Decumbent Lying flat on the ground but with the tip of the stem or flowers curving upward.

Disk flowers The cluster of tubular, rayless, generally five-lobed flowers, characteristic of the sunflower family.

Entire Undivided, with a smooth, continuous margin.

Epidermal Pertaining to the outermost cell layer of nonwoody plants.

Fascicle A bundle or cluster of leaves, flowers, stems, or other plant parts.

Filament The threadlike, anther-bearing stalk of a stamen.

Filiform Thread shaped; may refer to stems, leaves, flowers, or other plant parts.

Fimbriate Fringed with hairs.

Floret A single flower of the grass or sunflower family. Grass florets include the immediately subtending bracts.

Follicle A dry, generally many-seeded fruit that develops from a single pistil, opening when ripe on one side along a single suture.

Frond A fern leaf.

Funnelform Widening upward from the base more or less gradually.

Glabrous Without hairs, but not necessarily smooth.

Glaucous Covered with a whitish or bluish, waxy or powdery film.

Glochid A barbed hair or bristle.

Glume One of the usually paired bracts at the base of a grass spikelet.

Glutinous With a gluelike exudation.

Herbaceous Not woody.

Hispid Covered with bristly, stiff hairs; rough to the touch.

Hoary Covered with white down.

Hyaline Colorless, translucent, and transparent.

Inferior ovary An ovary growing below the calyx.

Inflorescence A cluster or other arrangement of flowers and associated structures on a plant.

Involucre A whorl or group of bracts subtending a flower or a group of flowers.

Keel The two lowermost, fused petals of many members of the pea family; also, a prominent dorsal ridge.

Lemma The lower, generally larger of two sheathing bracts subtending a grass floret.

Lobe A rounded segment or division on a leaf or petal margin or on another plant organ.

Margin The leaf or petal edge.

Midrib The central vein of a leaf or other organ.

Node The joint of a stem, or the position on an axis or stem from which structures such as a leaf arise.

Nutlet Any small and dry nutlike fruit or seed.

Ovary The ovule-bearing part of a pistil that normally develops into a fruit.

Ovule A structure within the ovary that contains an egg and may become a seed.

Palea The upper, generally smaller of the two sheathing bracts subtending a grass floret.

Palmately compound Compounded into two parts; usually referring to leaflets.

Palmatifid Cleft or very deeply divided into lobes that spread like the fingers from the palm of a hand.

Panicle A branched inflorescence in which the lowermost or inner flowers open before the flowers at the tips.

Parasite An organism that benefits from a physical connection to another living species, often harming the host.

Pedicel The stalk of a single flower or fruit.

Peduncle The stalk of a flower, fruit, or inflorescence.

Pendent Suspended, drooping, or hanging.

Perianth The floral envelope, composed of the calyx and corolla together.

Petal An individual member of the corolla.

Petiole A leaf stalk.

Phyllary An individual bract of an involucre that subtends a flower head in the sunflower family.

Pinna The primary division of a pinnate leaf or fern frond, or leaflet. The plural is *pinnae*.

Pinnate Featherlike; having similar parts arranged on opposite sides of an axis.

Pinnately compound Made up of pinnate leaflets.

Pinnatifid Pinnately cleft or divided into narrow lobes.

Pinnule A secondary division of a pinna.

Pistil The female organ of a flower, comprising the ovary, style, and stigma.

Pistillate Having pistils but not stamens; female.

Pollen The fertilizing, dustlike powder produced by the anther, containing the male gametophyte.

Pubescence A covering of soft hair or down.

Raceme A simple, unbranched inflorescence of stalked flowers that open from the bottom to the top.

Ray flowers The outer, often three-lobed, showy petal-like flowers at the edge of a flower head, characteristic of the sunflower family.

Reflexed Abruptly bent or curved downward or backward.

Reniform Kidney shaped.

Rhizome An underground, more or less horizontal stem, distinguished from a root by the presence of leaves, buds, nodes, or scales.

Rosette A radiating cluster of leaves generally at or near ground level.

Runner A slender trailing shoot that takes root at the nodes.

Salverform Having a slender tube, with an abrupt spreading throat.

Saprophyte A plant usually lacking chlorophyll that lives on dead organic matter.

Scape A leafless floral axis or peduncle arising from the ground.

Seed A fertilized and ripened ovule.

Sepal An individual member of a calyx, usually leaflike.

Sessile Attached directly by the base; without a stalk.

Seta Bristle or rigid, bristlelike body. The plural is *setae.*

Sorus A fruit dot or cluster of sporangia (reproductive cells) on the underside of fern fronds. The plural is *sori.*

Spatulate Spoon shaped; like a spatula; rounded above and gradually narrowing to the base.

Spikelet The smallest aggregation of grass florets and subtending glumes.

Spinescent More or less spiny; spine tipped.

Sporangium The spore-producing organ in nonseed plants. The plural is *sporangia.*

Spore The minute, dispersing, reproductive unit of nonseed plants (ferns and fern allies).

Spp. Abbreviation of the plural of *species.*

Stamen The male reproductive structure of a flower with a stalk-like filament and pollen-producing anther.

Staminate Having stamens but not pistils; male.

Stigma The receptive part of a pistil on which pollen is deposited; generally terminal and elevated above the ovary.

Stipe A leafstalk of a fern or of a pistil.

Stolon A runner or horizontal shoot that is disposed to root or to give rise to a new plant at its tip or nodes.

Style A stalk that connects an ovary to the stigma.

Subglobose Somewhat spherical or rounded.

Subsaline Somewhat salty but not excessively so.

Subsp. An abbreviation for *subspecies.*

Subtend To occur immediately below and close to another structure; often used to describe the relative positions of bracts, petals, and leaves.

Superior ovary An ovary that is free from and growing above the calyx.

Ternately compound Compounded into three parts, such as a clover leaf.

Truncate Severely attenuated, appearing cut nearly straight across at the base or tip.

Tubercle A small, wartlike protrusion or nodule.

Tuberous Bearing or resembling a short, thick, fleshy underground stem used for food storage.

Umbel An inflorescence, often flat topped, with three or more pedicels that radiate from a common point like the rays of an umbrella, characteristic of the carrot family.

Var. Abbreviation for *variety*

Viscid Sticky or glutinous.

Whorl A group of three or more similar structures (e.g., leaves, flower parts) radiating from one node.

ART CREDITS

Line Illustrations

DICK BEASLEY 24, 31, 34, 37 (bottom), 39, 44, 45, 46, 71, 78, 79, 80, 81, 90, 91, 95, 96 (top), 98 (top), 99 (top), 107, 108 (top, bottom), 116, 128, 131 (top, bottom), 135, 139, 144, 160, 161 (bottom), 162, 166 (top), 179, 182, 194

TOM CRAIG 47, 49, 57, 58, 98 (bottom), 115 (top), 133, 170, 186 (bottom), 192

ROD CROSS 33, 70, 101, 124, 189, 208 (top, bottom)

HELEN G. LAUDERMILK 52, 94 (top), 123, 129, 161 (top), 167, 172, 184

SHUE-HUEI LIAO 25 (bottom), 27 (top), 32, 35, 37 (top), 63, 65 (top), 86, 89, 92, 94 (bottom), 96 (bottom), 99 (bottom), 106, 111, 115 (bottom), 117, 119, 145, 151, 152, 157, 166 (bottom), 169, 171 (top, bottom), 186 (top), 187, 190 (top, bottom), 191, 193, 197, 200, 203 (top, bottom)

BILL NELSON 21

STEPHEN TILLETT 25 (top), 27 (bottom), 53, 54, 82, 112, 136, 156, 180

MILFORD ZORNES 65 (bottom), 138, 176

Color Photographs

BRUCE BALDWIN 22–23, 24

LARRY BLAKELY 103 (bottom)

BROTHER ALFRED BROUSSEAU, SAINT MARY'S COLLEGE 80, 121 (bottom), 138, 152, 156 (top), 185

CHRISTOPHER CHRISTIE 56, 61, 110, 133, 172 (top), 184, 191 (top), 204 (top)

WILLIAM FOLLETTE 79, 82, 87, 89 (top), 113, 156 (bottom), 169

JOHN GAME 26 (bottom), 30 (top, bottom), 32 (top), 39 (bottom), 70, 91 (bottom), 99 (left), 118, 139, 162, 195 (top), 196, 207 (bottom)

STEVE JUNAK 26 (top), 46 (left), 83 (top), 86, 94, 188, 198 (top)

ROBERT ORNDUFF 73 (bottom)

JON MARK STEWART ii–iii, vi, xiv–1, 27, 28–29, 32 (bottom), 33, 35 (left, right), 36, 37, 38, 39 (top), 40, 41 (left, right), 42, 43 (top, bottom), 44, 45, 46 (right), 47, 48 (top, bottom), 49, 50 (top, bottom), 51, 52, 53, 54, 55 (top, bottom), 57, 58, 59 (left, right), 60 (left, right), 62, 63, 64 (top, bottom), 66, 67, 68–69, 72, 73 (top), 74, 75, 76, 77, 78, 83 (bottom), 84, 85, 88, 89 (bottom), 90, 91 (top), 92, 93, 95, 96, 97, 99 (right), 100, 101 (left, right), 102, 103 (top), 104, 105 (top, bottom), 106, 107, 108, 109 (left, right), 111, 112, 114, 115 (top, bottom), 116 (top, bottom), 117, 119, 120 (left, right), 121 (top), 122, 123, 124, 125, 126–127, 128, 129, 130 (top, bottom), 132 (top, bottom), 134, 135 (top, bottom), 137 (top left, top right, bottom), 140, 141, 142 (top, bottom), 143, 144, 145, 146–147, 148, 149, 150, 151 (top, bottom), 153 (top, bottom), 154, 155, 157, 158, 159 (left, right), 160 (top, bottom), 163 (left, right), 164 (top, bottom), 165 (top, bottom), 166, 167, 168, 172 (bottom), 173, 174, 175 (left, right), 176, 177 (top, bottom), 178, 179, 180, 181, 182, 183 (top, bottom), 187, 189, 191 (bottom), 192, 193, 194, 195 (bottom), 197, 198 (bottom), 199, 200, 201 (left, right), 202 (top, bottom), 203, 204 (bottom), 205, 206, 207 (top), 209 (top, bottom), 210, 211

INDEX

Page references in **boldface** refer to the main discussion of the species.

Series Design:	Barbara Jellow
Design Enhancements:	Beth Hansen
Design Development:	Jane Tenenbaum
Composition:	Impressions Book and Journal Services, Inc.
Text:	9.5/12 Minion
Display:	ITC Franklin Gothic Book and Demi
Printer and Binder:	Everbest Printing Company

ABOUT THE AUTHOR
AND EDITORS

Philip A. Munz (1892–1974) of the Rancho Santa Ana Botanical Garden was professor of botany at Pomona College, serving as dean for three years. Diane L. Renshaw is a consulting ecologist. Phyllis M. Faber is general editor of the California Natural History Guides.

CALIFORNIA NATURAL HISTORY GUIDES

Field Guides

Sharks, Rays, and Chimaeras of California
David A. Ebert. Illustrations by Mathew D. Squillante
0-520-22265-2 cloth, 0-520-23484-7 paper

Mammals of California
Revised Edition. E.W. Jameson, Jr., and Hans J. Peeters
0-520-23581-9 cloth, 0-520-23582-7 paper

Dragonflies and Damselflies of California
Timothy D. Manolis
0-520-23566-5 cloth, 0-520-23567-3 paper

Freshwater Fishes of California
Revised Edition. Samuel M. McGinnis.
Illustrations by Doris Alcorn
0-520-23728-5 cloth, 0-520-23727-7 paper

Trees and Shrubs of California
John D. Stuart and John O. Sawyer
0-520-22109-5 cloth, 0-520-22110-9 paper

Pests of the Native California Conifers
David L. Wood, Thomas W. Koerber, Robert F. Scharpf, and
Andrew J. Storer
0-520-23327-1 cloth, 0-520-23329-8 paper

Introductory Guides

Introduction to Water in California
David Carle
0-520-23580-0 cloth, 0-520-24086-3 paper

Introduction to California Beetles
Arthur V. Evans and James N. Hogue
0-520-24034-0 cloth, 0-520-24035-9 paper

Weather of the San Francisco Bay Region
Second Edition. Harold Gilliam
0-520-22989-4 cloth, 0-520-22990-8 paper

Introduction to Trees of the San Francisco Bay Region
Glenn Keator
0-520-23005-1 cloth, 0-520-23007-8 paper

POST
OFFICE
WILL NOT
DELIVER
WITHOUT
POSTAGE

Return to:
University of California Press
Attn: Natural History Editor
2120 Berkeley Way
Berkeley, California 94720